Awakening the
GIANT Within

A Personal Adventure into
the Astral Realms

Greg Doyle

BALBOA.
PRESS
A DIVISION OF HAY HOUSE

Balboa Press books may be ordered through booksellers or by contacting:

Balboa Press
A Division of Hay House
1663 Liberty Drive
Bloomington, IN 47403
www.balboapress.com
1-(877) 407-4847

Because of the dynamic nature of the Internet, any web addresses or links contained in this book may have changed since publication and may no longer be valid. The views expressed in this work are solely those of the author and do not necessarily reflect the views of the publisher, and the publisher hereby disclaims any responsibility for them.

The author of this book does not dispense medical advice or prescribe the use of any technique as a form of treatment for physical, emotional, or medical problems without the advice of a physician, either directly or indirectly. The intent of the author is only to offer information of a general nature to help you in your quest for emotional and spiritual well-being. In the event you use any of the information in this book for yourself, which is your constitutional right, the author and the publisher assume no responsibility for your actions.

Any people depicted in stock imagery provided by Thinkstock are models, and such images are being used for illustrative purposes only. Certain stock imagery © Thinkstock.

Printed in the United States of America.

ISBN: 978-1-4525-7420-2 (sc)
ISBN: 978-1-4525-7422-6 (hc)
ISBN: 978-1-4525-7421-9 (e)
Library of Congress Control Number: 2013908462

Balboa Press rev. date: 5/30/2013

To my fellow human beings

INTRODUCTION

Where do I begin …
to relate to you an adventure that has awakened me from a slumber,
that I never knew I was having.
How can I possibly describe to you the hues and sounds and textures
of dimensions so vast and so alien,
yet so strangely comforting?

On the morning of March 13, 1999, the day after the death of violin virtuoso Yehudi Menuhin in Berlin, something very strange happened to me in the little apartment in Vienna I shared with my Austrian girlfriend. I had been in the capital for the past seven years or so trying to make my way as an orchestral conductor after studying the art there many years before. It was a hard slog, though, in that direction, and I just wasn't making the breaks I needed in order to cement a genuine and workable career. Having to resort to teaching English as a second language was starting to take the edge off an already compromised existence, as the torpor of "struggling artist syndrome" had well and truly begun to set in.

The art of meditation was a saving grace that I would practice daily in that tiny one-bedroom apartment. My mother had introduced me to the discipline many years before during my early years of tertiary music study in my native city of Melbourne, Australia. And those years had surely warranted it! The book *Relief Without Drugs* by the Australian psychiatrist Ainslie Meares was the opening of a creaky wooden gate into a garden I'd never known existed. It truly was the discovery of a new sense to me, and it literally helped me survive and succeed in those very difficult and trying years.

And so I knew that there was something … *else*. Or rather, I could sense an inner quiet that seemed somehow greater than me. But nothing could have prepared me for the realms I was about to enter on that fateful and wondrous Saturday morning.

This book is an attempt to recount to you some of the unusual experiences I've had over the past thirteen years or so, particularly in relation to the out-of-body experience, or *astral travel/projection* as it is often called. These experiences have not only ushered in a whole new paradigm of existence for me but have also shed light on the true nature of our reality, the concept of a constant and guiding presence, and the inexplicable force of the true meaning of faith.

A window into the divine mind, astral traveling has literally altered my cells; or more correctly, ignited the spark of being that was always there, but I didn't know it. It is a sense that lies within us all. It may be dormant, but it's there, just beneath the surface, waiting … waiting … waiting.

In full circle,
I was born into flesh,
spent years rejecting it,
and have now returned home to it
in full embrace of its power, its joy,
and its infinite breath.

CHAPTER 1

Shudders

There's light coming from the direction of the window. I'm awake; it's woken me. But it can't be the sun. We live in a mezzanine apartment. We're too low to get the sun.

I'm out of my body and moving very fast down a tunnel. So fast, like water gushing down a hose: twisting, turning, bending.

I'm in a landscape. It's real. I'm floating, still without body. Perfect vision. Barren, dry land. I see massive structures: tall, slender towers widening out to broad disks at the top. Huge and too modern. This is real. So it exists: there are others. This is not Earth.

When you leave your physical body, it's a remarkable thing. Your senses sharpen extraordinarily. Your ability to focus your thoughts and tune in to your surroundings is both effortless and forensic. You merge with surroundings, situations, people; you *know* what is happening. Normal 3-D reality pales in comparison; it just lacks the clarity, the sensation. That's why, for a time, I became quite addicted to venturing into this new state of being. It became an all-consuming natural high. And it changed me—for good.

To bring this into context for you, I need to take you back a little earlier in my life and share with you some of what had shaped me up until that point of no return.

When I turned thirty—around seven years or so before the light first took me from my body—I found myself living in Vienna in the middle of a turbulent year's musical study, experiencing the peaks and troughs of a volatile relationship with the city and its culture. This included my Serbian conducting professor, a new language, and (against all good and hardy common sense) my Italian landlady, who had just happened to become my girlfriend. In a rare and lucid moment of reflection, I envisaged life as a boxer dog, with me the ever-surprised-looking rag doll caught in its jaws, being summarily and comprehensively yanked side to side, top to bottom. Sure, it appeared I was living the European cliché—the somewhat naïve and hitherto sheltered boy from Down Under, keen and shiny-faced, seduced a little too easily by the aroma of spaghetti sauces (that really do smell a little too good) and the promise of all that comes with it, in a chocolate-box setting of art and culture that really was a bit *too* civilized, and pretty.

In our gorgeously renovated *Altbau* Viennese apartment—of course, just around the corner from where Schubert once lived— silence would erupt to full fury in seconds. All it took was an errant or mislaid and misinterpreted remark, and languages would be set all a-clash midair before falling to the floor all sullen and cracked. And you could really set your watch to the tide of these performances. After yet another customary weekly bout, I came to a sudden and lucid realization: *Life is what happens to you when you're planning your life!* Plain and almost dismissively simple, yet nonetheless relevant and subtly profound, I sensed the merest suggestion of an opening, a crack of light, like the release of an ancient splinter that had occupied a prematurely weary and distracted mind. I knew that I was somehow separate, to a degree, from the ongoing drama of my life. On relating this revelation to friends, I would be reminded that John Lennon had said it first and that I'd actually misquoted him, in that he said "Life is what happens to you while you're busy making other plans."

For some reason, this reaction doubly perplexed me. I felt it further supported the notion of the human experience standing inexplicably outside of itself. The point I was making was instantly lost to the clever and verbal world of statistical accuracy rather than actually being considered, and my realization, coming from the "mere mortal" that I was (as in: *not famous*), seemed somehow unable to carry enough weight to actually hit the ground and exist. What a peculiar feeling! The earth under my feet was eggshells, and I seemed to be speaking into a perpetual vacuum. Where was I?

On returning to Australia at year's end, the sensation of separation intensified, and I felt myself to be very lonely and depressed. I came to realize that I had actually been this way for a very long time, and I spent many hours alone, lying in bed in a strange and dark limbo. I was in the fortunate yet isolated position of "sitting" a house for a friend, and so I had very few bills to pay. This afforded me the luxury of time to investigate this immense and heavy state further. And it really did seem all-consuming and impenetrable.

I slowly began to make out shapes in the story of why I was "this way." I began to really hear my own breath. Certain hands and faces and names would draw genuine fear and anger from me, somewhere deep within and seemingly all at once. While I knew this to be logical and reasonable according to the particular traumas I'd experienced in the past, these energies seemed somehow different, as though enlivened by some unearthly blood to snatch at and grab and taunt me.

The beginnings of a conducting career, a new living situation, and the too-well-oiled cogs of the civilized and banal machinery—of having to work in a job that you don't necessarily want but kind of have to, to pay the bills because you've been unable to get enough of the kind of work that actually appeals to you—ever gently and forcibly took me back under its kindly concrete wing and mocking gaze to reenter the world anew: uncooked, uncorked, and decidedly unable.

And a lovely time was to be had! Sure, I was a world away from the circus of chaos and delight that had so lovingly earmarked my European debut, but why not shake a few tail feathers of my own while suffering the vast, yet captured and calculated landscape of this urbane and plenteous land? In short, it was time to shake things up; time to see who was really running the game here. It was time to play fuck-ups.

Strategy number one was to sleep, or attempt to sleep, with basically every girl I knew. That went quite well—probably about an 85 percent hit rate over the following twelve months, with a three-month interim while my Italian girlfriend came to visit. Oh, I was honest! If there was a double-up, I'd let them know. You see, by this stage, and as an essentially shy person, I'd actually all but given up on love. Not totally but almost.

Strategy number two was to strip back and intentionally under-hype any contribution I would make professionally. For example, in the world of music, it's the norm to really ham it up and overaccentuate what you actually mean to communicate. The bigger the character, the more huff and puff you exude, and the more important-sounding you make yourself out to be, the more impressive you'll come across. Not always but most of the time. I rejected all that; I was simply over the whole "emotional sham" thing and hence became ultra-minimalistic—definitely to the detriment of my career.

Strategy number three was to push my body to the limits. Just what was this whole "body suit" thing anyway? Running one day and swimming the next, plus a few weights each day would soon see both my knees taken out of action, literally within a few steps of each other.

Oh, this life—what an odd and curious play! So emotional, so real, and so bruising. So hurrying and forceful, with so little caress.

Occasionally at night, while sleeping in the old and creaky weatherboard house I was now sharing with a musician friend, I would sense an energy coming forward from the wall near the fireplace approach my bed and lean over me, in the pitch dark of that lonely and saddened bedroom. Its face would watch me for a time, and with its long curled neck hovering over my turned-deliberately-the-other-way, frightened, and too-stiff-to-breathe hunkering sweat-heap of a body, it would gently whisper: *Greg … Greg …*

Who was I?

5

*　　*　　*

Having effectively and neatly dismantled my life, my heart, and my self—and having left a girl I may have cared for (but was too numb to really know) sobbing and alone in my old and lost bed—I decided to brave the furnace of Europe once more. Half-heartedly and full of mock purpose, I set sail once again for Austria, to try to ignite a barely simmering conducting career and live out the continuing saga of my on-again, off-again relationship with my very own Mother Italy. Her first words spoken gently in my ear as we drove home from the airport—"Do you think this was a good idea?"—could not have been delivered to any greater effect. Punch-drunk and bewildered, I instinctively knew that I had to play this out, whatever "this" was. For some reason and as clear as day, I could see the train from *Petticoat Junction* blowing its smokestack (in full and glorious black-and-white) and gleefully charging my way—head on. The world has such a strange humor.

Needless to say, it was a tough landing, with all sorts of demons being hurled overhead, lassoed, and exorcised over the following year or so. Little by little, I began to realize just how stressed I really was and how much I'd fallen into the default and feverish role of the perpetual self-litigator, having to constantly prove my point or cement my standing in some way or another on any particular issue that came up between us. And come up they did! I felt like the goggle-eyed two-year-old who is utterly and obsessively immersed in the world of hammering back down those colorful and randomly popping-up blocks, while all a-dribble and head all a-shake in seeming obeisance to some mysterious source of fervor and conviction. Forget actually looking up and around at life on Earth; this was infinitely more challenging and engrossing, this strange and all-consuming need to be understood and in the right. I was in a perpetual shudder and a continuous fit, in a straightjacket of my own exquisitely suffocating tailoring.

And it was then that I saw it for the first time.

As I literally walked out of the door of that relationship, for the first and last time, I felt the tightly hemmed jacket that I'd mistaken for my life lifted and shaken from my contracted form for just the briefest of moments, to reveal a clarity and lightness of being I'd never known or at least couldn't remember knowing. I felt somehow suspended outside of myself, in that refreshing and light evening rain shower that will be forever imprinted in my memory, and something irrevocably altered within me. Through all the tears, introspection, and discomfort that were to follow, those few glittering seconds of mysterious joy would act as a beacon and unerring compass to my future bearings in this new and emerging landscape of fog and hope.

What was it really, this clarity, this glimpse into something free from any kind of suffering? *And could I get it back?*

A few months before the breakup, I'd had an unusual dream. Well, it was actually more than a dream; I've come to know these things as *visions.* They present themselves differently from dreams in that a very clear picture of something is shown to me, while sleeping, with a precise energy or message attached. And at the very moment I see it, my consciousness is somehow cleared of any mental white noise or dream interference, rather like the stillness of a Zen sand garden, tended to with all the calm and smoothness of deliberate and loving intention. In this vision, I saw the face of a very good friend of mine, Monika, in total clarity, hovering above my own, smiling easily and openly into my eyes. As I emerged gently to full waking consciousness, the vision and message remained wholly intact: *I knew that I loved her—and that one day I would marry her!*

From one moment to the next, my perception of a good friend I'd known for almost two years had shifted most viscerally within me. I confusedly called her the next day to ask her if she felt there was also something in her mind between us. An odd yet strangely comforting conversation followed, with us both semi-probing and semi-revealing that something serious, deep, and long-lasting might well be awaiting us at some point in the not-too-distant future. We both hung up slightly confused and embarrassed, and we never spoke of it again, remaining friends for a good six months longer (we were both still in relationships at the time) before finally coming together.

This was my first rock-solid encounter with what I have come to term *guidance*. An indelible etch upon the hard drive of my mind. And when I experienced that fleeting sense of joy between the pain of leaving and resolving the tumult of that most combative and engaging relationship, I knew it had sprung from this same mysterious well.

Over the next while I began to see a psychotherapist—coincidentally a friend of Moni's—who really helped clarify my situation. My face was just so lined and racked with ... *something*. My spirit felt so bruised and hurt, and my body so taut. *And so many tears ... so many tears.* I felt like I had been running against the direction of a conveyor belt for the longest time, caught in the strangest of tape loops, repeating over and over the same emotional wringing match. Why had I identified so much with this ever-warring and haunted persona? *What was I really on about?* Through the therapy, I could feel myself being pulled to the surface of something new and enticing. I could just make out the glimmer of a different sun through the thinning depths of a still turbulent yet receding murkiness, and I was determined to feel its touch.

I soon broke the surface and gulped my first breath of that sweet-scented and rarefied air to the sound of laughter, *Moni's infectious laughter*. As clichéd and overly romantic as it may sound, the intonation and texture of it woke me up from this strange and morbid stupor I'd inhabited for the longest of times. It was the sound of chimes tingling, tickling, and thawing a frozen and contracted heart. I remember actually being quite shocked at the time and thinking, *What is this? It sounds so ... real.*

You see, I'd finally come home.

CHAPTER 2

The Invitation

Wormhole (noun): *Physics* a hypothetical
connection between widely separated regions
of space-time.—*Oxford Dictionaries*

G limpsing into these lightened spaces was like separating calcified vertebrae. It was sudden, electric, and I knew that freedom was to be found there. It was time to reclaim my life from the addictive and life-sapping roles of reactivity and victimhood that had somehow and somewhere along the line bagged me unawares and taken me hostage. It was time to discover who I really was. For I now genuinely sensed there was more to me than I had formerly given myself credit, as strange as that may sound.

I began to meditate again and came in touch once more with the tender heart-space and stillness that had kept me afloat during those difficult earlier years of tertiary study. Once my lifeline in a time of struggle, I now realized that this state was in fact closer to who I really was than the perpetually stupefied and powerless rag doll I had identified with. It was time to "defragment" myself and see what was left.

And it was painful. To look into yourself and release pain and anger—and attempt forgiveness, whether of yourself or others—*hurts*. There is no other way. As you let go, you relive, and that is both the price and the potential stumbling block for so many who seek to shed the mantle of their alleged drama and heal themselves. In the end, it's a choice. My very last words to my Italian girlfriend (who was deal-making and pressing all the right guilt buttons right up until the final, fatal sword stroke) were uncommonly clear and prophetic: "*I have to save my own life.*" Ringing from the same eternal well-spring as Moni's tinkling, thawing laughter, once voiced and set to wing, I felt an ever-so subtle loosening of the manacles around my wrists and the beginnings of something new—and infinitely more inspiring.

I began to write down everything I was feeling. That really helped. There just seemed to be so many conflicting emotions battling for higher ground within me, everything bubbling to the surface in a jostle to be released, and that included physical pains. Such a fermented, raucous brew! One fine morning, I awoke to a mysterious and agonizing body-folding stomach pain. I could barely walk. After being rushed to hospital and receiving what was presumably a relaxant shot to the area, the pain subsided, never to be experienced again. Another occasion found me doubled over in a distracted and mind-numbing moan of lower back pain, which had built up over the previous few weeks. As I exclaimed "That's it, I can't take it anymore!" the pain seemingly took heed and immediately vanished from the scene. *Strange.* Yet another occasion found me taking an aching right shoulder to a series of practitioners without any success, until I lucked upon a certain craniosacral/energy healer who seemingly precipitated a major energetic change within me. More about the details of that later, but it would appear that the time was ripe, and I was somehow primed for the beginning of the journey of a lifetime—or perhaps the journey to end all lifetimes.

I'm asleep, on my back, with my hands folded behind my head, and it's just before dawn on Saturday, March 13, 1999.

There's a ball of light coming from the direction of the window. I'm awake; it's woken me. But it can't be the sun. We live in a mezzanine apartment; we're too low to get the sun.

Keep your eyes closed.

Triangles of light forming in my forehead. Making a circle. Very bright and very white. My heart feels unusually good.

An invitation?

I accept.

There's wind roaring in my ears. It's loud.

I'm out of my body and moving very fast down a tunnel. It appears ribbed and is an orange-brown color. I can see, but I have no body. So fast, like water gushing down a hose, twisting, turning, bending.

I wonder if I can leave when I want, at a certain point in the tunnel. As soon as I have this thought, I'm out— seemingly to the right.

I'm in a landscape. *It's real.* I'm floating, still without body. Perfect vision. Barren, dry land. I see massive structures: tall slender towers widening out to broad disks at the top.

Huge and too modern. Lights on in some of the hundreds of windows. It feels like dusk. This is real. So it exists: there are others. This is not Earth.

And so it began—my adventure into these other realites, and one that has become a defining journey of experience that has altered my perception of what it means to be human. You see, *we are not alone.* And I don't mean that purely as in the whole extraterrestrial thing, although ...

What I'm talking about is that there seems to be a very present, active, and largely invisible world, or energy, that underpins and influences our own three-dimensional one. And when you start to experience this world consciously, you seem to activate something within your own body and mind that enables you to interact with it more fully. It is as though it is waiting for your acknowledgment to truly come alive.

As I've alluded to, I feel these senses within me were awakened primarily through meditation and the unconscious desire to want to know more. The meditation techniques I had used to this point were aimed purely at relaxation, as I had found that simply becoming less reactive to potentially stressful situations was helping me remain calmer and happier in my day-to-day life. Also, as I mentioned earlier, I was on a deliberate quest to strip myself back and rid myself of the emotional armor I'd gathered along my life's path. But nothing—*nothing*—could have prepared me for *this!* I didn't seek to have an out-of-body experience, nor had I actually been aware of the existence of such a thing up to this point. In fact, when it first happened, I was utterly confused as to what had happened. What was this clearer state of being? What was this light and this loving energy that had flooded my heart and had instigated it all? *Where did I go?* And this ... *wormhole?*

With every grain of my being, with every subatomic particle of my body, I knew that I had just visited another planet—*out of absolutely nowhere!* This had simply *happened.* A light had come, awakened me, invited me out of my body, and taken my consciousness down a tunnel and into the atmosphere of an alien world. The buildings were not of our technology. They were vast and contained beings—as evidenced, I felt, by the artificially illuminated windows. And this now was fact! In a matter of seconds, I knew that intelligent life existed elsewhere than on Earth. And this was not a question I had previously obsessed over in any way. I hadn't asked for any kind of revelation to show itself. In the space of a few magnificent and earth-shatteringly real moments, my world had irreversibly altered its rotation and set me on a course that was unknown, uncharted, and immensely inviting.

And the strangest thing of all was that this very alien world somehow felt like home. How can I justly portray to you the feelings I had as I hovered there in an atmosphere that was in no way Earthly, watching in absolute diamond-precision clarity over this vast vista of dry arid land with these enormous towering structures directly in front of me? Why was it so *moving?* When I returned to my physical consciousness and opened my eyes, I shed quiet tears of ecstatic joy. But why? Something immense had released in me, that much I was sure of, and I had returned somehow greater than when I had left. It was as though a giant truth had resounded within me, gifting me with a tremendous sense of relief—but from what, I wasn't sure. I had in some way or another touched home.

I also now knew, beyond any kind of conviction, that it was possible to exist outside of the physical body.

The very next night as I lay down to sleep, the light came again. Immediately. It seemed to collect all the fragments of light behind my already closed eyes and concentrate them into a focused circle right in the middle of my forehead, and *whoosh,* the wind began once more. This time, however, I didn't feel any kind of loving energy accompanying the light. It all seemed too sudden and out of my control. So I freaked out and aborted the trip by throwing my eyes open. *What was happening here?*

Now this is not the sort of thing you share with people. They're going to think you're crazy. Fortunately, Moni, my then girlfriend (who is now my wonderful wife) realized quite quickly that something major had happened to me. And she listened; I was very grateful for that. We did have a close friend at the time, my former psychotherapist, who held a meditation circle once a week, and I described to her what had happened. She suggested it was *soul travel* that I'd experienced, and she handed me a book on the subject. I was relieved to put some kind of label on it. It made sense—kind of. It was at least a start.

So … soul travel. Apparently, your soul could leave your body, taking your consciousness with you. It sounded a little too religious or esoteric for me. Too untouchable. What I'd experienced had been so kinesthetic—so *real*. Could there really be such a spiritual element to all of this?

I believe so. A few nights later, it happened again, and I became conscious once more while sleeping. What actually woke my mind up was the whirring of an internal engine, seemingly within the space of my actual physical body. It's difficult to accurately describe, but you sense these energetic pulsations throughout your body—an almost ticklish yet very pleasant sensation. You feel your body become weightless as the vibrations quicken slightly. And you are totally conscious as this process kicks into gear. Then it is as though your body is lifted and *carried*. That is what I was alluding to earlier when I stated that there are other forces at work, guiding our energies and experience. For I do feel I've been privileged to see through a window into our workings: that of the human experience in interaction with what we perceive to be our only reality, this so-called 3-D one.

On this particular occasion, after being lifted from my physical body, and after what seemed around ten seconds of my invisible body moving though some kind of empty space, I materialize in what feels like a medieval inn, with a man and a woman sitting with me at a corner table by a window. All wood and stone and low beams overhead. Quite cozy, really. I sit there dumbfounded as they both start to tell me about myself and make a little too much sense. I decide to exit the scene—*a bit too real.*

So now I'm back in bed. I sit up: *what was that?* Unreal! Well, actually … *not.* That's the problem. I'm back to sleep quite fast, though, and *whoosh*—I'm out again and back to the same place, seemingly to the mild amusement of my two newfound acquaintances. This time, I observe them closely. They seem so … *normal.* So calm and focused. Very smooth skin. The guy appears in his late thirties, she in her forties.

They're very relaxed and in loose, nondescript clothing. This time I ask the questions:

"Where am I?"

"We're in Gwyneth, one of eight worlds."

"As in Gwyneth Paltrow?"

"Yes. Similar but not quite." They seem to find this mildly amusing. "The next world is Selwyth."

"Right. And who are you?"

"We're your guides—for now."

"I'm outta here."

And so I am. Back in bed. Eyes wide open.

This whole thing was too clear. Same place twice. *Gwyneth Paltrow?* Plus the whole guide thing: too New Age. Now these details are those I remember verbatim. A lot more was spoken and asked, but these are the aspects that have stayed with me as verbal memory. You must remember, I was in a degree of bewilderment at the time and busy processing the whole experience. The thought of documenting it all for a future book was the furthest thing from my mind. However, the *energy* of all that occurred in these meetings has stayed with me and that, I believe, has been the most transformative aspect.

You may be thinking, "Oh, go on—it's just a dream!" But I ask you: Are you dreaming this? Now? *That's* the sticking point. And this is where you perhaps, dear reader, have to suspend your notion of reality. As this moment is real for you, so was that for me. In fact, more so. More distinct, more focused. As someone who has gained quite a degree of control in dreams—so-called *lucid dreams* (which are not real)—I can say that these experiences *were real*. As real, for all intents and purposes, as this present moment.

Interestingly, the county *Gwynedd* in Wales (pronounced similar to *Gwyneth*), as I later found out, seems to have had some mystical significance during the Middle Ages. I had no knowledge of that before this experience.

Regarding the New Age feel to the whole *guide* thing, I hadn't read up on such subjects at that stage. *Guides* were not part of my vocabulary then—and so I found it all the more remarkable that this actual word was used. In fact, I would still to this day call myself a healthy skeptic when it comes to any kind of mystical phenomena. Firsthand experiential evidence has always been and remains my yardstick of what I deem to be *truth*.

So. Back in bed. Body still vibrating like mad. I'm interested. Let's see what happens.

Eyes closed … I'm gone. Immediately (and I wasn't even tired). I'm lifted again and travel blind through some kind of space. I suddenly find myself sitting in a grassy field with the same female guide. It's beautiful here! The light is bright and low, and there is a slight breeze caressing the long grass. The whole scene seems to emanate its own light. She proceeds to tell me about energy and auras, and how to see them. And I do—I see the colors around everything, including her. Distinct colors; sharp outlines. I'd heard of auras and of people seeing them, but I'd never paid much attention to it. But this! This was fantastic!

Overwhelmed by the situation—this being the third visit

and all—I decide to push the boundaries a bit, dismantle the whole thing. After all, this is *my experience* … isn't it?

Without going into detail, I make a rather sexually provocative comment toward the guide just to see how she reacts. After all, I'm thinking, *Who is this person? Why am I here? What's actually going on?*

I will never forget her response. She gives me a wry yet gentle grin, looks me in the eye for a while, and then says, "Greg, I've been watching you for some time." Then she seems to close in on me, her face just inches from mine. "Why are you so sad?"

CHAPTER 3

Unseen Forces

Mystical (adjective): concerned with the soul or
spirit, rather than
with material things.—*Oxford Dictionaries*

Okay. So up until this point, I'd been more interested in the mechanics of the dimensional shifts than the content of what was actually being said or communicated to me. Was there a relevance to what this supposed guide was telling me? Was this a form of, dare I say it, *spiritual* help?

The intensity with which she had asked me had sent me back to my bed with a jolt. I literally *felt* her question reverberate through me as a pulse of energy, deep into the interior. It was as though it had imbedded into my core—a quivering arrow, demanding my attention, demanding an answer.

Was I sad? Sure, I'd had my share of disappointments over the years, with my career not going as I'd planned. I'd had my dark nights of the soul, as we all have, and had experienced loneliness, depression, and isolation. I'd fallen victim (and perpetrator) to the toxic clamps of loveless relationships, as many of us do. But I felt this question was aimed at something deeper within me. Just where that place was, I wasn't sure. Which led me to thinking: what was I? Not just *who* but *what?* Something more, perhaps, than the mere individual named *Greg Doyle?* I began to sense something stirring within me, a visceral intelligence muscling its way to the surface.

My next adventure would shatter my belief system for all time.

I had been raised a Catholic, but I never really got the whole "cross" thing, that he died for "our sins." I didn't feel I was that bad, and I sometimes felt guilty for not feeling more guilty. As a child, I'd thanked "Peter God" for years at dinner, albeit quizzically. I thought he may have been a relation to Peter Rabbit, with whom I felt great kinship and understanding.

I didn't like most churches. They made my skin crawl when I went into them. But some, I could recognize as meditative spaces, although heavy. But one thing I did kind of believe was that we had our life—our one life—and then we went to some kind of heaven (or someplace really, really nice) to exist in a higher state of grace, whatever that was, and that was it. *Schluss.* Out. Hmmm …

The engine again. I'm awake, yet my body's asleep. Lifted, turning, weightless. Silence. Nothingness. A sense of waiting … watching … I sense a question emerge.

I want to see me.

It's me! My face directly in front of me, just a couple of feet away! As clear as day.

A slide show in 3-D. I'm getting younger! Wind in my

ears with each change of picture. Eyes remain the same, never moving. I'm a baby. Now I'm gone.

It's an old man with a brown weathered face; creases everywhere. Mongolian? Slides again. And wind. Eyes never move. A child, a baby, gone …

An African, not so old. He looks powerful, scary. A medicine man? Arms out in front. He's wearing lots of stuff. Eyes so intense but still never moving. I'm scared, but I stay with it. It won't hurt me. Wind again and now he's a baby; now he's gone.

A non-human. An elongated head. No hair. Tall. Thin, very thin. Wind; getting younger. Eyes stay the same. The background … that's not Earth! This is too much. I'm freaking out now. Good-bye!

As I open my eyes in bed, I hear a friendly laughing voice sing *Intermis-sion.*

What … on Earth … was *that?*

To be honest, I had no idea what any of it meant. The 3-D nature of the experience and the ever constant position of the eyes had been the most fascinating aspect of it all. And the whole alien thing? I also found it interesting that I had posed the question—or rather, it had emerged from me—during the weightless waiting period, and I felt that there must have been some relevance to what was asked and what was shown. I was shown something. That, I felt sure of.

It wasn't until weeks later that a friend suggested that it may have been some kind of past-life regression. I didn't actually believe in past lives, but I was intrigued enough to be open and do a little research into the matter. It fit. In fact, it fit very well.

And so I had the feeling that I had come face to face with *me!* Not only have I existed before (and these were real people I saw, not just ideas of people) but I have also existed as a non-human, as an extraterrestrial—and I know exactly how he looked! After I let the shock of the experience subside, I felt an aspect of the crust of my mind loosen its resistance to this belief and begin to absorb the new paradigm of the possibility of a multidimensional existence. It was the subtle half-turn of an ancient, rusted, and internal key. And the fact that we all, presumably, have this capacity hardwired within us, to call up a 3-D record of our soul's journey that may well reside within our own energy field, was, to put it mildly, astounding.

This notion of the sadness being deeper than just me or my situation here, in this life, paired with this greater picture of who I really was—*what* I really was—seemed to make some kind of sense. I began to feel that I was a lot more than the dramas of my life. When I tuned inward and closed my eyes, I could sense an energy that was untouched by the daily trials and victories. It was ... an expansion.

During the next while, I found myself often out of my body, experiencing other lives. One particularly memorable example:

It's raining—beautiful, big warm drops. I'm walking on a dirt track, and the air feels so vibrant and moist. I'm feeling euphoric. I put out my palms and watch the heavy warm drops bounce off them. I enter an old stone building and go through the doorway to the right. The men sitting in towels all look up at me, puzzled, through the steam. Something tweaks. I go back out and enter the other door. There are women there. I look in the mirror and study my face. This is

24

bizarre: absolute detail. I'm a woman in my late forties, and I look Spanish.

I also discovered another way of entering this other realm. During a lucid—or conscious—dream, I would look around for an object that seemed particularly detailed or stable in its appearance. I would then focus in on it with all my awareness, and more times than not I would find myself zooming in through the object to another 3-D realm. Pertaining to other lives, here's another example:

> I'm in a room. I realize I'm dreaming. The things around me waver when I look at them; they change form or break up. Scanning around, I see a painting on the wall. It's big, abstract, with vivid colors. It's set in a very solid, ornate, textured wooden frame. I focus all my energy into it. The painting expands, and with a loud, accelerated rush in my ears, I'm through it and into a real, old, musty wooden hall. There's incense in the air and symbols on old, colorful hanging materials. It looks like Chinese. I'm shouting orders at a group of men in a foreign language. It's a dormitory of some kind, and I seem to be in authority. My robes are long, red, and tattered, and my fingers are brown, worn, and elongated. As I walk around, I look at things … so many strange objects. Why is it that my mind is in this body—in it but not of it?

I can only relate these experiences to you. I don't see it as my role to interpret them or make sense out of them for you. But I can tell you, just as I have gained these experiences, I have gained a sense of *knowing*. I now know that I am much more than this life. I know that my energy, or soul, has experienced, will experience, and is perhaps experiencing many other lives right at this moment. In fact, I know we are here on Earth for that very reason, to *experience*. And this kinesthetic intelligence has enabled me to release any fear of annihilation, death, or nonexistence, for it simply does not—*it cannot*—exist. But more on this later. Let's get back to the mechanics of what was taking place.

I had found a few books on astral traveling and reckoned that's what I was doing. I was somehow projecting an energetic double into these alternative realms. But how and why was still a puzzle to me. Had my energy field been somehow altered to enable this, or was it just a random form of awakening? The answer may lie in an experience I had a month or so before my first outing. Or it may not. But I do feel this is worth relating to you, as something astonishing did occur.

*　　*　　*

My right upper arm had been sore for some time. I had helped move a baby grand piano up a narrow flight of Viennese steps (silly me!) some months before and was just unable to shake this throbbing, annoying pain below my shoulder. I'd had a reconstruction in that shoulder ten years earlier, due to a car accident, but this pain felt unrelated.

After trying a couple of chiropractors without success, I found myself visiting a craniosacral therapist who had been recommended to me. She told me that what I had was an energetic block in my arm, and she freed it by holding my arm and moving it very gently in various directions, or so it seemed. That was it! One treatment, done, gone. Well. I asked her, should I come back, do I have any other blocks? She said a couple more treatments certainly wouldn't hurt; that I'd definitely feel better for it. She seemed okay, so I did.

The second treatment … oh yeah … quite nice. I didn't really feel much—just a bit of movement running around my body. It was relaxing, though. As she had suggested one more visit, I thought okay, I'll honor that.

The next one was a cracker! As she was very gently moving my head to one side—so slowly, as though her hands were being guided by subtle movements in my own neck—I went into what could only be described as a kind of full-body spasm. Energy roared into my solar plexus, my knees contracted up to my chest, and I involuntarily rolled over onto my right side into a quasi-fetal position. I felt a surge of pure anger rip through me. I could hear my own voice, as if from a distance, screaming out obscenities through me. Pictures of things past flew by my eyes—scenes and situations (even odd things, like an old packet of balloons I'd had as a child) poured past at lightening speed. The therapist seemed mildly concerned and asked me if I was all right as she backed away from the table. While continuing to scream, I was somehow able to reassure her that she was in no danger. I knew, deep down, that this had to out.

Apparently, this reaction is what is known as a Somato Emotional Release in the craniosacral-therapy world. She had triggered an almighty release of stored-up negative energy—built up, perhaps, through abuse I suffered as a defenseless child, and maybe even through past-life accumulative trauma as well? Whatever you call it, this was powerful. My body knew it, and I knew it.

After this treatment, I actually felt very strange. I'd imagined I might feel freer—that was to come later—but for the moment, I felt like a stranger in my own body. Very uncomfortable. I guess that energy, albeit negative, had been part of who I was, or part of who I *thought* I was. But I did know that this was somehow a good thing taking place. I decided to follow up and went back a week later. Things were to get very interesting indeed.

During the next treatment she took a look at my jaw and told me that I had been unable to store and process aggression correctly, that my jaw had not developed as it should have and was letting this energy flow through too easily, inhibiting my ability to express it. Some people store too much aggression in this area, as evidenced in many men with very heavy jaws. And so she proceeded to put her fingers into my mouth and prod away at the gums. Quite startling, really. There she was, both hands in my mouth firing energy through her fingertips while very gently manipulating the whole jawbone.

That night, I was in pain. My whole mouth felt like it was on fire. I could actually feel it stretching from within. My gums were burning and so uncomfortable. I was relieved to fall asleep. Little did I know that the most startling was yet to come.

The next morning, upon awaking, I was greeted by the face of a black wolf just inches from mine. Eyes closed, eyes open again, *still there!* Piercing almond-shaped green eyes, a white chin, and growling. I will never forget it. I got out of bed and had a shower. *Still there!* It was a holographic, translucent head of a wolf, in full detail, following my gaze wherever I looked, whatever I did, and always growling.

This really upset me. I had things to do, and it wouldn't go away. I broke down. I was in tears. Had I gone mad? For three days and three nights, it was my constant companion. Of course it must have been related to the treatment, but in my panic I didn't figure out the connection. I'm so grateful for my girlfriend's support at that time, as it was literally impossible to function normally.

Now, here's where it was all heading. I'd been having a bit of a dispute with my flatmate over an unpaid bill. Or rather, I *should* have been. The tension between us had been building, but he was a rather furtive kind of chap, not given to confrontation. Neither was I. But he was adept at the art of passive aggressive warfare, and I wasn't. And so the whole affair was eating me up. Whatever had taken me over railroaded me into one humdinger of a fight. It emerged as an eruption of hot-headed yet clear-thinking argument, at least to my mind. Raised voice but not losing it. It did feel different. In the past, I'd had so many problems with expressing my anger, I would just shut down and not be able to express myself as I'd wish. But on this occasion, I felt I'd been able to remain lucid in the thick of it. Yet here is the really astonishing thing: after the row, the wolf proceeded to lick my face, turn away, and walk back a few meters or so before curling up in a ball in the corner of the room. And so that was it. Over. Not quite.

It did seem that he'd served as some kind of council, as some kind of friend. The licking at the end … And it made sense in the light of what had preceded it in that last craniosacral treatment. But the actuality of it. *The wolf.* How could that be? What or who was behind it? Could it have been triggered by my own energy field? So vivid, so real, for so long. Or was I mad—*seeing things?* The black old face, the green eyes, the wizened, white chin …

Not a week later, I was sitting in a room waiting for my first students of the day to arrive. I was teaching English at the time, in Austria, to adults learning it as a second language. As I looked up from my lesson plan, in walked a woman wearing a T-shirt with a picture of exactly the same wolf—the face exactly as I'd seen it! I was absolutely dumfounded. Speechless! The hairs on the back of my everything stood up; in fact, my whole body pulsated with energy. I just stared at her for a while before greeting her. When she sat down, I had to underplay my reaction a little, but I did manage to splutter out that I'd seen that wolf before. She seemed to take that onboard okay. And she was dressed … *differently*. All in green. I asked her what she did for a living. She said she was a Reiki master—that she moved energy around to help people heal. Then the rest of the class came in.

Okay. So what was the connection here? The treatment, the stored-up aggression, the *wolf*, the Reiki woman—all within, say, ten days. The same wolf on her shirt could not have been a coincidence. I became obsessed with trying to find who had drawn the wolf. I scoured the Internet. Hours. Days. I couldn't find it. She told me she had received the T-shirt as a gift some time back. But someone must have drawn it: *the very same wolf.*

Interestingly enough, I started to notice Reiki books in shops. I had always felt there was something more to our hands. The same woman recommended me a teacher. Ten years later, I would become a Reiki master.

CHAPTER 4

You've Really Gotta Get Out More Often

Astral (adjective): —of, connected with,
or resembling the stars: *astral navigation.*
—of or relating to a supposed nonphysical
realm of existence to which various psychic
and paranormal phenomena are ascribed,
and in which the physical human body is
said to have a counterpart. Origin: early
17 century: from the Latin *astralis,* from
astrum 'star.'—*Oxford Dictionaries*

N ow remember, these craniosacral treatments that triggered the holographic wolf to appear preceded my first travel out of my body. So presumably, something *had* shifted within me. I was also still meditating most days, simply because I found it calming and enjoyable. Then there was also a dream I had a short time before it would all begin, featuring the woman who ran the meditation circle, who had been my psychotherapist, and who I now knew as a friend.

In the dream, she was sitting on the ground in a circle with some Indian men. She was talking with them, apparently about me, from the way they seemed to be motioning. In the center of the circle was a large golden ring. After a time, one of the men told me to concentrate on the ring, to go inside it with my mind, which I did. And it was the most beautiful feeling. Once inside, everything disappeared—including me. My mind was floating in this enormous void with this absolutely heavenly music playing. As clichéd as it sounds, I remember it to be harp music or something similar. There I was, just lolling around in the void listening to these indescribably beautiful sounds.

Eventually I awoke, trying to invoke the feeling for as long as I could. But as I said, this was a dream. I was not conscious that I was dreaming at the time, nor was I in any way controlling the content of it (that was to come very soon). But this dream did somehow hark back to the earlier vision I'd had, with Moni's face hovering so clearly above mine. It also had the power of the wolf in it and the scent of those earlier episodes of lightening. I recognize it now as a spirit dream, where beings and energies of the invisible realms come forward to touch us and prepare us in some way to experience and develop further.

* * *

So. Back to the future. Up until now, I had only traveled into other realms and experienced what appeared to be other lives. But the astral travel books that I'd read suggested that we were also able to access *this* reality outside our body—so we could effectively see ourselves sleeping or take flight and visit a friend. They suggested exercises to gain control over one's *astral body*, as they termed it.

One of the principal exercises was to imagine your body floating above you when you were in bed. This wasn't hard to do. I would imagine myself looking down at me from around six feet above and swap my mind's perception between the real me and the imagined me hovering above. I think the idea of this was to suggest to your mind that you could exist outside your body. Another exercise was to literally focus your eyeballs, behind closed eyelids, on the space between your eyebrows. This was the place where the light had first appeared and had taken me on my first "tunnel" outing. Various schools of mysticism referred to this spot as the *third eye*, one of the energy centers of the body linked with clairvoyance. If you could remain focused on this point as you fell asleep, the strain of the exercise would help you fall asleep consciously, thus achieving the great paradox: body asleep—mind awake. This was the ideal state to achieve an exit in real time, that is, in *this* reality.

I began to play around with these techniques with varying degrees of success. I found when I fell asleep focusing on my brow, at the very moment my body would enter sleep—and it did take some time, often up to an hour and a half—a window would open up just above and between my eyes, like a screen. More often than not, I would be so shocked that I would jolt awake as soon as this occurred. Why didn't everyone know about this? Why was this information relegated to the realm of mystical religions and/or fruitcakes? This was real—a sense we have all lost, perhaps?

On one occasion, the woman who had professed to be my guide

appeared *and waved!* On other occasions, the windows would open up into other realms, as before, which was interesting but not what I was after. I wanted to experience being a ghost in *this* realm. I wanted to float out of my body and see myself asleep. I wanted to see what was happening when we all slept.

I found that real-time body exits were not being activated directly from the techniques I was using. However, things did start to move up a gear a few weeks later, and more times than not, it would happen just before dawn. I would first feel the pleasant engine pulsation start to activate. Then I would open my eyes, thinking nothing had happened. I would look around the room—all was as it should be. But the engine sensation would still be there ... a little strange. Below, some examples from three separate occasions.

Okay. It's happening again: the vibrations. I open my eyes. Nothing. I go to turn on my side. This feels strange. It's hard to describe. I feel myself "rotating" to the side ... too effortless, like being lifted a little and turned. Am I still asleep?

The vibrations. I think I'm still asleep. I'm going to get out of my body. I feel my left arm detaching itself from ... itself. And now, the right arm. Both pointing up in the air. I start to sit up, pulling out. Almost ripping out. But I'm stuck around the stomach. Can't move! I wake up. Body still lying down. Almost there.

The vibrations. This time, don't move. Just focus on the window. I can get there. Yes! I'm floating. But no body. I'm tiny; a speck. I'm falling toward the corner. I can't seem to hold it. I'm falling into the corner of the room and onto the floor.

So this was the pattern of things: almost getting out but not quite. The trick was to realize when I was asleep or not and then to develop my astral legs (or wings?).

Not long after, I found myself staying at a hotel in Munich. That night, I went to bed early and did every exercise I could in preparation for a successful out-of-body journey. I even asked for help from my guides. Hopefully they were tuning in.

Nothing has happened. It's just before dawn. I'm awake and getting up to go to the toilet. I get to the bathroom door. Something feels amiss. I turn around and there I am, lying in bed! Eyes closed, asleep. I walk toward myself but not too close. I feel a pull. The strangest feeling to see yourself that way. Scary, actually. I turn around. A woman walks though the room. She's naked and walks like a zombie. I ask her who she is. She says, "I'm English," and exits through the far wall. Right. I walk up to the wall to put my arm through it. It doesn't work; my arm hits the wall. I relax and do it again, imagining it going through. It works. I actually feel the wall as my arm passes through it. Fantastic! I go to walk through. I sense the wall as I pass through it. Two people are in the next room, naked, hovering above themselves in bed. I jump straight up, through the ceilings, through the floors.

I'm above the hotel, hovering. Focus. I want to visit my girlfriend back in Vienna. The universe sounds a giant *om*, while traversing or being suspended in a giant black void. I'm flying, like Superman, really fast. Wind in the ears; it's all a blur. Now I'm still, and there's a very tall building below me. Very detailed. I'm through the wall of our bedroom back in Vienna. My girlfriend is asleep, hovering just above her body. I say hi and she opens her eyes. She looks drunk, happy. I ask her to come with me. She says "Great!" and then closes her eyes again, asleep. I'm being pulled back. Awake in bed in Munich.

Yeah, baby! The big one. Gold!

The next morning, over breakfast, I see the English woman sitting at a table, dressed. Also, the two people from the room next door. A couple of weeks later, I see a photo of Vienna's newly built Millennium tower in a newspaper—the city's newest, tallest landmark—and a wave of energy surges through my body as I recognize it to be exactly the building I observed astrally from above, having never seen it before in the flesh.

So I'd done it! I had left my body in real time. This was, for me, the ultimate proof that we can exist outside of our bodies. But once again, more questions presented themselves to me: who, what, and why? Who or what is behind all of this, and why is it happening? And as I said earlier, the sensation of flight was as though I was being lifted. By whom or what? Being shown the skyscraper in vivid detail as I flew over it—as though the process was deliberately slowed, so as to aid in later verification of the location and experience—by whom or what? People seemingly hovering above their bodies when they sleep—*why?* Are these their astral bodies? Are they *dormant?* And *why me?* My definition of reality was already substantially eroded at this stage. Was it to deteriorate totally? I couldn't possibly leave it at that. I had to look into this further.

I would often fly out into space. This was particularly enjoyable. To see the Earth get smaller and smaller. To look around and zoom in on distant star systems. To see the universe populated and thriving, to sense its life force. To see the throbbing of consciousness all around us. And it was a very positive feeling. I'd often come back from these outings feeling overwhelmed by a sense of joy. I suppose knowing we're not alone on our planet is perhaps something we all crave, deep down. Is it? I ask you. For I now *know* that we are not alone. So far, far from it! But can you believe it, that we are not alone? What within us has been so drenched with the impossibility of it all, of other beings on other worlds? Why do we recoil at the thought of it, either out of absolute disbelief or of dread and fear? Why is the theme regarded as science fiction—not to be taken seriously?

There are answers, of course, as there always are. Perhaps there are those who are served by us believing we are alone or under threat. "Go on—make another film on the subject. Make 'em scary. Make 'em out to be monsters. Keep it in the realms of fiction." Why? Is contact so bad?

Incidentally, around a week after my first light-led, tunnel, out-of-body experience, I happened upon the Carl Sagan–inspired film *Contact* in my local video store. The experience of Jodie Foster's character as she travelled down what could be only be described as an inter-dimensional wormhole and was shown the lights of an extraterrestrial city—to which she responded, "Okay, so they exist," or words to that effect—was so similar to my own experience that it moved me to tears upon watching it. How could this be? Such a coincidence! Not only the content and loving sentiment of the film

("You were shown this, because this is how contact is always made") but the sheer timing of strolling past a local video store and seeing it in the window within a week of my experience.

Was this, in fact, what it was all about? Contact?

But can you also understand how utterly isolated this made me feel? What if I truly had been shown an extraterrestrial culture, which I believe I had? *No one would believe me.*

It also threw up the question that perhaps others had experienced this method of introduction. Otherwise, where did the inspiration for the film come from? Pure fiction? I'm not so sure. Years later, I wrote to one of the creators of the film who was a scientist (and also responsible for the pivotal wormhole sequence) to try to glean an insight into his motivation for creating the scene as he had, but I was unable to get a response. Yet in my mind, I felt that someone else *must* have experienced this phenomenon and method of contact.

But more on the existence of others later. For now, what was fascinating me was the aspect of being aided in the out-of-body experience. I also found that when it appeared too dark to see anything, I would ask for light and then I could see. Once again, I had the feeling someone or something was at hand, helping the whole process along. And if that was the case, then perhaps we were meant to be developing this sense—perhaps we were meant to have multidimensional awareness. I decided to test this theory the next time I was out.

I'm high above the city. I'm going to fly … that way; fast. My arms are by my sides as I feel the acceleration kick in. It's immediate: as soon as the desire emerges, I go. A tremendous force of wind on my face; it's all a blur beneath me.

I sense something at my ankles. It's difficult to do against the current, but I carefully and slowly bend my neck back to the right to look at my feet.

How can I describe this? There is a pair of hands, almost transparent, holding my ankles. And they're not alone. There is a person attached. He's translucent, almost invisible. It's just the outline of a body. It's like it's made out of glass or crystal—all angular surfaces. He's actually flying me while flying himself. And now he speaks. I can't make out the words. They sound so distant, so alien, as though they're crackling through from another place entirely. His voice sounds metallic, as though spoken through a machine of some kind. But I understand the meaning of his words: *You shouldn't be seeing this; this is something you don't need to know.* With a degree of difficulty and pain, I strain my head against the force of the speed and wind to face forward again. I sense the pain is a slap on the wrist, a slight punishment for daring to look.

Could this really be true, that we are not actually meant to know of this assistance? It does tie in to what I hinted at earlier, that there is a whole other reality underpinning our own, and that we are guided through much of our mostly unconscious experience on this planet. Do you really think that when you sleep, that's all you're doing—sleeping? Synapses randomly firing and the body and mind purely resting and rejuvenating—do you think that's it? Let me put this to you: When you sleep, you too journey out of the body; you too are shown things. You just don't remember it all, as you are not conscious during the process. But what if we can be conscious? What

39

if we all have the potential to wake up? Would the human race alter its way of thinking? Would our priorities change? Would we, dare I say it, stop killing each other? I put it to you that the capacity is there in all of us. When we begin to wake up to what we truly are, life takes on a whole new perspective.

You know that feeling when you've awakened from sleep with a new feeling or an inkling of a different approach to take? Perhaps you've had a dream that was particularly vivid? You'll never know the full truth of it until you activate this astral body of yours. I've been lucky: I seem to have been given a free pass. But then again, not really. I do believe regular meditation and the focusing of my mind internally has made this particular process of self-discovery more accessible. Without the desire to clear yourself—to know what's really there within you—this innate sense of ours may remain unfulfilled, like a bud that has never flowered. I know I'm starting to sound clichéd, even a little preachy, but having seen what I've seen, having experienced everything I've experienced, I feel this is too important not to share with my fellow humans.

It seems that we truly are guided by essentially unseen forces when we astral travel. In that way, we are helped. But are we to actually recognize this? The astral realms are ours to explore, to experience and to learn from; in fact, to help us expand our consciousness to a fuller awareness of what it means to be human. But it seems the mechanics of this—for example, the translucent being flying me—are to go unnoticed. Or are they? I say this because the very urge to look back was an impulse of guidance in itself. It's rather like looking into a mirror through another mirror and so on. Ironically, I felt that the act of seeing this was a message to me that we should not feel that self-determination was not our own. The urge to fly in a certain direction was mine, and the carrier was purely responding to that urge. Perhaps his rebuke was to tell me to stay focused on what I was doing, not to obsess about the mechanics of it? I really didn't know. But this I did know: more questions were being raised, and I was determined to find out as much as I could.

CHAPTER 5

The Buddha in the Belly

As the doctor pronounces him dead, I know
I've borne witness to something remarkable.
In the last moments, I could sense his essence
drawing away from his physical body, leaving
only a shell. As the nurses go about their duty
and the room fills with those mourning, the
chubby little Buddha in my belly loses it. He's
gone from an open watchful smile into an
irreverent fit of hearty, sidesplitting laughter.

It gradually became easier to enter these other realities and to
recognize when they were upon me. I would wake up in bed,
normally just before dawn, having prepared myself at the beginning
of the night. As always, the sensation was pleasant when the process
began: a gentle whirring of an internal energy field, the stirring of

an invisible force that was within me. What purpose did it play, this hidden body of mine?

It has been written that what is known as the lower astral dimension is populated by lower entities and that not all inhabiting these realms are necessarily enlightened beings or particularly *nice*. I can attest this to be true. Without getting into an intellectual discussion on this theme, as the purpose of this book is relating my own experiences to you, I have occasionally been accosted by unusual and very ugly creatures as I cross the threshold of realities, particularly in real-time exits. One memorable example:

Okay. I open my astral eyes, slowly. I sit up in bed. My body detaches smoothly. At the end of the bed is some kind of monster! About four feet tall—half animal, half human, and hideous-looking. Hairy and fat, waving his arms around at me and growling menacingly.

I'm shocked but not scared. Something inside me shouts out "Fuck off!" Which he does, thankfully.

Often, toward the beginning of a journey, creatures will spring into my path or just appear in front of me. This is an interesting phenomenon. They will hiss, threaten, throw things, or just generally glower at me. But this situation has lessened substantially over time, and I think many exist because the collective human psyche has feared them into being, and so they have taken residence in these lower realms. I say *lower* because these other realities seem to operate at varying vibrational densities or frequencies. Others, I believe, simply exist there and prey upon the fears of unwary travelers for kicks, or so it seems. Perhaps they act as a warning to those venturing into these relatively uncharted waters: "Don't bring your fears with you, otherwise you'll attract more!" Whatever they are, they do exist but can be dealt with quite easily. Just tell them, in any way you wish, to go away, and they will … usually. (But that's for another chapter.)

I don't mean to freak you out or scare you in any way with these accounts. I'm just telling it how it is, how it has been for me. Any research I've undertaken on any of these themes has occurred after the fact. As you can imagine, when something so out of the ordinary happens to you, you instinctively want to know if others have shared that same experience. After all, we're all human—we're made of the same stuff. Interestingly, do you know what that stuff is? It's *star matter*. It all derives from that almighty primordial explosion. And when you think of how you as an individual are created, there's a startling parallel. It's said that all the information in the universe— everything that has ever happened there (or here)—is stored in the universe. What if that information is also stored within us? We are of the same matter, after all. What if our bodies themselves are our greatest store of knowledge, a master Wi-Fi connection to the center of all creation? Now I'm waxing, but you can see what I'm alluding to: our cells contain our stories—everything. It's up to us to find a way to access them. I believe this is what my journey is all about.

Returning to the subject of threshold entities: these have been very well documented throughout human history, pertaining particularly to the appetite of men.

I'm just beginning to fall asleep, with consciousness still intact. Body gone … and there's a woman sitting astride me, really going for it! She's physically attractive with dark hair and wearing a brief yellow leather outfit. There's another woman next to her, also with black hair but wearing black leather. They're having a time of it and shrieking to themselves. It doesn't feel good. I let them know that I see them and tell them in no uncertain terms to leave. They seem shocked at my animation and, after a moment's conference, they fly off.

Referred to as *succubi* down through the ages, these energies/ beings prey on men's sexual desires, apparently draining men of their energies or vital force. I know it sounds far-fetched, like a cross between a *Buffy* episode and *Dr. Strangelove*, but they do exist, seemingly in the lower astral planes. It's a subject most men won't talk about, but many will know what I'm referring to. They often see them as a flash just as they wake or fall asleep. And they wonder at how real it felt. It's nothing like a nice dream. It's very real, and there's an ugly vibe associated with it. When you kiss these entities, you'll wake up immediately with a disgusting taste in your mouth. Whatever purpose they serve, I'm unsure of—but I do know that they try to take something from us that can deplete us of our vitality. They show themselves to be attractive, but they are not! Remember, everything is energy, and you can very easily distinguish between what makes you feel good and what doesn't. There is quite a difference! I really urge men to try to identify that difference and wake up to it. Identify them or the feeling, and tell them to go away. *And they will!*

On the subject of energy, I'm often asked what I think it is. My answer: everything. A few years ago, I became acutely aware that our five senses, while naturally vital for our experience here on Earth, are not the be-all and end-all in terms of how we actually sense ourselves or interact with the world around us. They're in fact very basic and practical and external. Dependence upon them separates us from who we actually are—*what* we actually are. Great for day-to-day operations! Many instruction manuals exist, particularly in the fields of science and medicine: "Do that and take that and then this will happen!" All well and good, but I'm not a robot. I'm not a toaster. I'm much more than that! I am *energy*. If you close your eyes, do you sense it? The buzz. All through you. That's who you really are, *what* you really are. And when you tune in to it, constantly, it begins to feel acknowledged. It looks up from the chair where it's been sitting in a stupor for all these years, or perhaps lifetimes, and starts to remember what it is. Its eyes begin to glimmer in recognition, in hope. And it will give you the biggest smile imaginable,

He's always there inside me. I sense him in my belly. I'm not a Buddhist, but he sometimes looks like one of those plumpish cross-legged figurines you see in Asian discount stores. He's often leaning forward onto his knees delighting in so-called stressful situations, with that look of "What's he going to do next?" I've found the heavier the scene in human terms, the more he rolls around laughing—often literally, holding his sides. It can be quite off-putting when you're supposed to be reacting in a certain way to give a situation some gravity or drastic import. The "Oh, that's just terrible" line doesn't quite come off.

The trick is to go mad, to be out of your mind. For you see, this resource within you—which is your greatest counsel and ally—has nothing to do with logic or the parameters of understanding you have built up over the years. It's visceral, palpable, instinctive, spontaneous, and unerring. It's *knowing* as distinct from knowledge, and it will not fit into the neat, straightjacketed perception of your mind. I believe this energy or internal presence is what the mind is supposed to be. Free it, don't flood it! When I'm out of my body, I note that my memories are different. They're vast and carry less of the emotional weight of my waking mind. They're very open. And after I return, I do literally feel a sense of expansion, a broadening of awareness. I feel more *me*.

So it seems that astral travel, or astral projection as it is also called, exists as a tool to broaden one's awareness as a multidimensional being. We are helped out of our physical bodies, shown things, taken places. We have the ability to perceive the intent or the message behind the physical facades of what we encounter. And it would also seem that we are able to make contact with intelligence from other worlds. This next bewildering experience started out with a dream.

I'm walking along a track and notice a river close by. As I approach the river, I see an arched bridge crossing it. I cross the bridge and find myself entering a room that is lit up by a wall of square, multicolored panels. I greet someone who I appear to know well. I'm happy to see this person and I hug him/her enthusiastically. A little too much so, it would seem, as he/she pulls back, slightly abashed, from my advance. He/she is about five feet tall, bald, androgynous-looking, and wearing a silver metallic bodysuit. He/she then looks at me and says very clearly, "Let me show you something."

The internal engine. I'm awake. *Don't move, don't think.*

Laser lights boring into my head, seemingly into my brain. It's like I can see through the very tissue. So loud—in fact deafening, like a dentist's drill. Right there, with the lasers, from all different angles. It's going on for some time. This is really full on; too loud. On the verge of pulling out.

It's stopping. Objects now being shown to me. Many of them. Very clear, one after the other, as though on an invisible carousel. They seem to be very modern instruments or tools of some kind. I don't understand their significance.

They've stopped. What? I see four rounded corners—white—of a small screen, like you'd see through a video camera, being fitted into position in the upper right of my vision. Now there is some kind of data being processed very fast in the upper left corner of that screen. It occasionally pauses, but I don't recognize the characters. As the data is being processed, I feel a metallic tingling sensation in my head, above and behind my right ear, as though a series of tiny coins are being dropped in there, in incredibly rapid succession.

There's noise in the courtyard below; people speaking. Bugger! My body's waking up. It's over.

That was something else; something entirely different. It was the first time I'd felt the presence of some kind of technology interacting with me in the astral. And that it was seemingly alien technology only added to its other-ness. It hinted at the very first experience I'd had, down the tunnel into that alien world. Also, the fact that I had somehow been transported unconsciously from the dream preceding it. In fact, the initial dream may well have been forgotten had I not been awakened by these strange forces. The lasers, the drilling sounds, the objects, the juggling into position of the screen, the data transfer, the foreign hieroglyphs, the sensations in the brain: an alien intelligence was at work here. This, I was sure of. And it was working on me. But who, exactly, and why?

It occurred to me around this time that so-called alien abductions, particularly those that took place at night when the subjects were in bed, may well be astral phenomena. I would often feel the tugging on my feet and ankles as I was pulled out of my body during the night. This wasn't always a good feeling; it could actually be quite scary. But note that I now differentiate between *I* and *my body?* Throughout this whole process—call it what you will—I was becoming increasingly aware that I was a lot more than the vessel that housed me. And in so doing, I found I became more and more courageous in my astral venturing. More often than not, I would choose to go ahead with the expedition, in the full knowledge that I would always be safe, as I always was.

CHAPTER 6

The Others

I wake to the screeching cries of the jets. My internal engine comes alive and my heart thumps savagely. Body gently lifting and rotating now, and then accelerating to warp speed as they draw me out toward them—the others. I feel a sickly mixture of fear, recognition, excitement and exhaustion. Such strange science!

I often found myself on massive ships, surrounded by all sorts of people who generally looked like they were sleepwalking. I'd be watching it all but almost playing dumb, shocked by the enormity of what was going on. In many of these experiences, I had the feeling that it was a kind of parallel life, in that I would revisit many chapters of the same saga, continuing on from the previous episode like a television serial, except that the reflection in the mirror was mine and my earthly memories were totally intact.

The ships were run by a race of very tall—seven feet or more—

and very blond people. Their skin was literally white, but generally, they looked like us. They were very calm and thoroughly in control. It's funny, because when I have related this to friends, they think I've been watching too much *Doctor Who*. Even funnier is the fact that I don't watch that show at all.

In these scenes, I never heard the blond people speak. But they did have an intimidating vibe about them. I once tried to leave the ship, while being detained, through a hatch-like door that led on to a piece of land that didn't look or feel like terra firma. I was quickly pursued by a quizzically tall and very blond look. Never a smile. The information was clear in an instant: *You can leave, you can even take your own life … but we will always have access to your energy. And that is all we need.* I then became acutely conscious of a band around my wrist.

Now this really does sound like sci-fi, doesn't it? But this is how it was. I ask you to try to remain open as you read this and remember, the scenes were at least as real as your sitting there and reading this. I've had many particularly vivid dreams in my time, but these were not those. Nothing like them, in fact!

I would always know when one of these chapters was upon me from my astral body being awakened mid-sleep by the squeals of what sounded like menacing jets very loud in my ears. My own astral engine would gear up as I flew out to meet the craft. I would always see them as I boarded them: huge things. Way out of our world.

There was a definite hostage element to the whole experience—as though a sleeping aspect of my consciousness through its own passive complicity was somehow permitting itself to be herded, dominated, and in some way usurped by these beings. And it truly was on a massive scale: these ships were like small cities with thousands of human sleepwalkers boarding them. It often took all my energy just to remain conscious enough to stay with it, rather like treading water over an extended period of time with the eyes struggling to peep over the surface. Hence the sickly pall to the whole thing. Any surreptitious engagement with other humans would be furtive, fleeting, and generally unsuccessful, as they appeared zombielike in their gaze, vacant and altogether compliant. They would catch my eye and almost recognize something before collapsing back into the malaise, eyes lost. All advances I made were watched and noted closely by the silent others. Chilling stuff, actually.

You may see some parallels with the film *The Matrix*. And I would agree. Having not seen the whole trilogy—because funnily enough, I'm actually not that interested—it would appear that others may well be inspired by this phenomenon to create these stories. Remember, the collective human subconsciousness is powering much of our experience here, and as it slowly wakes from its slumber, aspects of the greater reality are beginning to reveal themselves as the veil of feigned separation starts to fade. And this was no fiction: the ships, the others, and the human hordes—*this was reality.*

It finally ended when I decided to speak up. Basically, I'd had enough of being herded there, even though I knew I could have aborted the reality at any moment. I had been trying to explain the status quo to a few of the other humans over the past few visits without much success, and so I decided to make a show of it, make a memorable exit. As we all sat in one of the huge mess rooms we were prone to do while waiting for our meals (to give them credit, the food actually tasted quite good, and the cutlery was excellent) with everybody chatting happily, albeit somewhat vacuously, the screams of what sounded like cattle being slaughtered were coming from a room close by. As the screams reached a climax, I stood up and announced, "We're next!" The blond attendees quietly shot me a collective look, while the "inmates," to their credit, did manage quite a stir. As you may well imagine, that was the last time I was invited to dinner. And understandably so!

You may be somewhat puzzled by my cavalier attitude toward it all, but do understand, my perception of reality, even this reality we all share *right now*, has been altered so dramatically over the last decade or so that I really do see everything and every experience as a paradigm of sorts. It's all purely a play of energy. And it's there, or here, to serve us in some way or another.

Dare I say it, I find the whole thing, including this life … fun!

❋   ❋   ❋

But it wasn't all bad out there. Far from it. On one particular occasion as I was backing away from the Earth, trying to keep it in sight so as to hold my bearings and not jet off to some unknown corner of a parallel universe, I came across what I felt to be the asteroid belt of our solar system. An awesome sight: a floating world of massive boulders suspended as if by some heavenly magic. As I closed in on one patch of the field—as if I were being pulled in toward it—I noticed several triangular craft parked up against the rear sides of a couple of the rocks. These were big rocks, mind you, but I don't feel the craft were that big. They were motionless, sleek, slate grey, and perfect equilateral triangles. After a moment's shock, I knew their role was that of protector: a form of galactic coast guard, if you like. And I knew they were protecting the Earth, but from what?

In the very next moment, a huge ship entered my vision from the right. It really was enormous when compared to the other craft.

It was white, the size of an office building, and emblazoned with black block-style writing toward the tail, which tapered slightly from the rest of the ship, making it look almost like a giant white whale. This truly was an awesome sight! And so, *so* real in magnificent 3-D, HD—no, ultra-HD—with the maximum possible pixilation allowed. I'll never forget the play of the cutting and intense white light from the sun as the ship cruised by. The writing on the side was clear and looked stenciled, similar to the style of our own military. It looked to me more like a mathematical code than any language and seemed to be made up of circles, dots, and lines—all with rounded corners. But I knew precisely the translation, in an instant: *Galactic Federation.*

Now this really was too much. Galactic Federation? Not only too embarrassing to relate to anyone but boring to boot! Straight out of some Spielberg film or a seventies *Star Trek* episode. Just plain unimaginative. But I knew it to be a fact. Pure and simple. When I got past the simplicity and apparent dumbness of it all, I began to wonder why I was so resistant to the notion. What in the human psyche made the whole Galactic Federation concept so laughable? Were we really so naturally blinkered—or were we, in some way, being manipulated away from truths from a culture that places more weight on fear and entertainment than the seeking of knowledge? Is money involved? Are we, in fact, the cattle?

Don't get me wrong; I love a good movie. And I was to gain an answer from this so-called federation before I left the scene. My question to them was this, and it was asked with a deep yearning from a place of separation that bonds all humanity: "Why are you not known to us, and why are we not a part of this planetary collective?" And as my body began to haul my consciousness back to its earthly awakening, I heard the words as clear as day, spoken in a calm and gentle male voice: *Because you continue to kill your own.*

Hmmm ...

We do, don't we? I remember growing up in Australia during the sixties, with war being reported on the television daily. I remember crying one evening during one of these reports. I remember a boy at school named Phillip Head saying, "Ah well, war is just one of those terrible things we have to have." I remember thinking, *Dickhead.*

And the very intense feeling I had on awakening from that particular travel was that this was a huge truth. In some enormous volume of an intergalactic encyclopedia would be the entry for *Earth:* "Division D planet, Solar System, Milky Way—carbon-based, human-incarnation platform (non GF member—*still kill own*), approach with extreme caution." And somehow I felt that warfare was the red card when it came to the adjudication. You see, it's not at all hot-blooded: it's calculated by those with power, with suits and ties. It's nothing to do with a primal urge to protect the physical, to stay alive in the heat of an attack. Its intent is cold, dishonest, and misleading. And it says something about a planet whose inhabitants gladly go along with it. Millions die in its grip, but it's somehow okay? Something we have to have? Is it?

A person goes to jail for killing another in the heat of fury, yet a country remains free for sending its children into so-called glorious, cold-blooded battle? I don't think so. And this is our Earthly inheritance. Rather like the inadequacies and shortsightedness facing policymaking of short-term governments, the human race believes wholeheartedly in its mortality. It fears annihilation on a personal, national, and global level. And that on a daily basis! What a strain! Imagine if we all knew that we truly were immortal—that Earthly death was not the dreaded fat lady singing after all. That in fact our lives are here to serve us; that beauty is in everything and everybody around us. That we are here to live!

I'm sorry if I insult some of you by not being more politically correct in my approach here, but in the same breath, I couldn't be more unapologetic. You see, there have been so many atrocities committed by the human race in the name of religion ("Thou shalt not kill?"), ideology, and nationalism; so much bloodshed and misery wrought at the hands of our so-called wealthy, clever people (our *leaders?*), that I think a little criticism here can be endured. For the message and clarity on awakening from this experience was so intense and urgent—and so *simple*—that I'm sure you can understand my impassioned plea on the subject.

The real war is within us: generations of inherited anger and hurt. Once we release it, we release ourselves and the planet. Don't you think Earth, too, has a consciousness? You know with each second it gets closer to the center of the galaxy, closer to its truth. We're in this together, spiraling through the universe like a whirling dervish, a dancing embrace of sound and light. And love. You know that's what it's all about, don't you?

* * *

As I mentioned earlier, I would often feel something tugging at my feet during the night. And it didn't always feel that good. After one particularly strange episode where I felt I was moved from craft to craft in a quasi-drugged state—and remembering very little—I awoke to find a pair of identical fresh moles on the outside of my left foot, directly below the ankle bone. Two perfectly round and very defined circles about a centimeter apart. *What magic was this?* When I've asked doctors about these marks, they can offer no explanation. Two identical, perfectly rounded … *whats?* And they're exactly parallel to the sole of the foot. Over the twelve years or so since they appeared, very little has changed except for the perfection of their shape.

It's hard to rightly explain, but I do think many things go on between our species and extraterrestrials. As clichéd as it sounds, many people are being used somehow for experimental purposes. But it is our choice to participate. I didn't feel comfortable with this sort of thing, and for a while I became very scared. I didn't want to close my eyes, nor could I watch or read anything to do with so-called aliens. I wouldn't sleep alone; if I had to, I would keep the light on. The dread when I would walk outside alone at night became unbearable. I remember on one occasion looking up to the sky at night and seeing, *feeling*, a dark patch fly toward me. I felt very strange for quite some time after that.

I eventually went to a Reiki master and friend who had trained me in the healing method to see if she could help me. She could. In her state of meditation, as she was applying the healing, she told me she could see or sense an artificial object in my forehead. She believed it was not Earthly and that it was some kind of chip. She saw it as translucent and rainbow-colored. I took it to mean that the object was *energetic*. And that was entirely what she meant: that the object was placed there energetically, in my energy body. Now, with everything I'd experienced over the preceding years, I didn't find that so far-out. I recalled the laser drilling and screen-fitting experience I'd had a few years before. I wondered if there was a connection. I asked her to get rid of it, which she did. And I've never had this kind of trouble since. But here is the really interesting thing: I felt a sense of loss. Over the next few days I could feel them bidding farewell to me; I could sense them in their craft, observing me and saying good-bye. And I was somehow sad, yet absolutely relieved, for I had to let them go to remain healthy. I found this whole process … *unusual*. And that's why I say that it's our choice to stay with the experience or not. You will feel a sense of loss, but you will get over it. Many of you—more than you realize—are suffering needlessly under the strain of this experience (and these experiences are real, despite the constant and puzzlingly aggressive campaign in the media to debunk them). But are you actually enjoying it? Do you need it to define you? Would you like to sleep well again? Are you prepared to let it go? If so, make the decision and get some help. I've never looked back, and *they* know to leave me alone.

I still like to make contact, but not in this way.

You must know, too, that the Earth is protected. We are being watched over by others who genuinely have our best interest at heart. Despite the frothing madness of a film industry that thinks otherwise—no, that would like *us* to think otherwise—we can come to no real harm at the hands of another race or alien species. So drop the feigned fear of contact once and for all, and release and lower the drawbridge of invitation with an open, fearless, and welcoming heart. Perhaps it's also time to drop the term *alien*, a word laced with connotations of fear, violence, and nonacceptance.

Perhaps it's time to join in.

CHAPTER 7

Michelangelo's Fingers

The huge moon is pale and red above me. The stars are distant. I close my eyes and feel such immense calm. Pure, unadulterated, space.

By far the majority of sorties into these other dimensions have been positive and uplifting. On one particularly memorable occasion, I found myself walking along a stony surface of a very quiet and peaceful terrain at night. There was no wind and the atmosphere felt somehow charged. You could almost feel the curvature of the surface as you walked, as the horizons were very close in all directions. Above me and to the right was an enormous moon, so close and red in the dim light. I don't think I have ever felt as peaceful as I did there. I remember just standing there for some time feeling absolutely elated. When I closed my eyes there was nothing—no tension, no fear or anxiety, no *effort*. And it became very clear to me while standing on this world so very far away that life was not a test; it wasn't a school. It was just what it is, *life*, to be celebrated and experienced.

Another trip found me walking through a surreal forest of leafless shrubs. Once again, it was totally peaceful; the light was very dim and the sky was a deep, deep violet. In front of me was a lake that seemed to be crystalline, almost metallic in nature, with a soft glow emanating from it. As I entered it, I could feel its energy rising up my body. But here is the remarkable thing: I could also feel this energy rising up my sleeping physical body at the same time. Two bodies, one consciousness. The sensation was very visceral, healing and rejuvenating. A baptism on a foreign world.

One expedition found me flying at high speed along an enormous river or fjord. I could see the shores—very green and treed—on both sides and stayed low to keep in contact and not zoom off into space. I soon noticed an arm of the giant river opening out to the right, and I could just make out something on the surface in the distance. It looked like flowers, large lotus flowers, all magenta and white—a field of them—gently rising and falling on the water's breath. As I neared the scene, I saw a pier amidst them leading to what appeared to be a Hindu-like temple on the shore: a beautiful, perfectly preserved, ornate, golden, stone temple. I landed and walked along the column-lined path toward the steps leading up to the opening. Not a soul was about. It was a truly exquisite scene, yet I wondered at the lack of anyone present. As I approached the steps, the already dusky light began to fade and the temple was soon gone from sight. What was this beautiful place? Why was I here? And why had the lights been suddenly turned out?

In these far-off places, my mind had space to breathe. I would often return with tears in my eyes, with a sense of ecstasy, deeply touching, beautiful, and unusual. Perhaps this separation from the collective Earthly consciousness enables one to sense with greater clarity. And if energy truly is everything, then to be away from the thoughts, hopes, disappointments, tragedies, excitements, desperations, and triumphs of the human drama, even for just a few moments, can be a wonderfully liberating experience. For our thoughts do create energy, you know—or more correctly, they *are* energy. Every thought you've ever had as well as everything you've ever experienced is imprinted in your energy field as it leaves you and floats out into the ether. And our energies are constantly meshing, bouncing, and interacting with one another. Imagine watching the Earth from space: its globe spinning all the creative human energy off like a great celestial spider; streams of ideas as light and sound, mingling and meshing with universal consciousness. As beautiful and awful as our creations may be, they are nevertheless the result of a highly emotionally charged species. A break from this circuit—a hiatus from the human maelstrom—is like a crack to our shell, releasing the automated and reactive and letting in the unfathomable and the inexplicable. A divine connection, perhaps? *Michelangelo's fingers* ...

And so this exiting of the world became a reflex, for me. Why wouldn't it? I couldn't wait to put my body to sleep at night and free myself from these earthly shackles. Up, up, and away! First the hum of the second body, then the exit, and finally the exhilaration of acceleration as I headed up through the roof and through the atmosphere with nary a glance behind. Until ...

I'm away. The acceleration is extraordinary. My arms are pinned to my side, and my body is corkscrewing slightly as I rocket out into the expanse. Extreme pressure and wind on my cheekbones, jaw, and forehead. But what's this? I feel a hand around my shoulder, a giant hand. The thumb on my left shoulder, the palm around my upper back, and the fingers around my right shoulder and upper arm. It's stopped me and now it's pushing me down, back down to Earth. I'm in its grip; it won't let me go.

Well ... first of all, *who or what was that?* Was it God? I don't think so, but someone or something—once again—was watching, and dare I say it, guiding. And that was it for astral traveling for some time; I just couldn't get out. I felt like a trapped tiger. I think my girlfriend was actually relieved, as she'd felt I'd been a little bit absent of late.

I found it very difficult to get around after that. Life became a cage, the color draining from the waking day (and the sleeping night). Stripped of these powers, I became unanimated, irritable, and depressed. This so-called reality was so bland compared to that other state of being. Where was the grace, the sense of humility, the fineness?

A few months later, I was walking along the street from a Viennese U-bahn station to the hospital where Moni lay under anesthetic, having just had her appendix removed. I was still confused as to my astral expulsion and absolutely terrified that she wouldn't wake up. As I crossed the busy street awash with the cacophony and chaos of construction, I began to hear the faint laughter of schoolchildren drifting over a high brick wall on the other side. I normally close myself off from street sounds, as I often find them too loud and overwhelming, but something different carried on these tones. They began to envelope me, all around and through me, lightening my being and soaring me into the moment, the much touted *now*. Time froze, and for a moment, for just the slightest sliver of a moment, I sensed the ecstasy of being once more. As I walked on, I knew that she, and I, were okay.

When I say that time froze, I mean that everything *stopped moving*. It happened again a few weeks later. At the time, we were renting an old house up high in the mountains a couple of hours out of Vienna. It was often under snow, and we could cross-country ski from the front door. I'd gone out on my own under one of those white glowing skies that you sometimes get, with the clouds just above, all kneading and radioactive. The snow was perfect—thick and fresh—and the air was crisp and still. It had just started to snow as I arrived at a steep decline in the forest track. Ahead of me lay a field, and the thickening snowfall with its big fat flakes started to glimmer in the glow. So quiet … As I looked around me in euphoria at this silent wonder, it happened again. Time stopped—I mean, *it really stopped*. The flakes hung suspended in mid-fall, and I could see all through the spaces between them. It was as though the Earth's great second hand had gotten stuck and before it had been tapped back into action, I had been able to see into the very mind of creation. In that eternal moment, I could truly sense the dance and felt my heart join in. Perhaps this reality wasn't so meager after all!

This was to happen a few times over the following weeks. Time just pausing at random moments, catching its breath, and enjoying the space. That word *space*, just what does it infer? Breaks, openings, gaps, breath, wonder, the unknown. The very thing I'd been yearning for, that sense of space, was in fact all around and through me— us—at all times. Weaving through our own dimension, and all that we are and do, is this place of extreme stillness, an access point to absolute awareness and universal connection. And the way to access this was to *listen,* with *all* our senses, including those we didn't even know we had.

Not long after this discovery of time gaps, the good old astral body started to crank up again. It was nice and most welcome. I'd never actually stopped doing the exercises, but I'd stopped obsessing over them and not being able to get out. The next outing was, indeed, a doozy.

Ahh … the engine. It feels good. My body's being lifted and somehow rotated. Think nothing and see what happens.

I'm moving. It's dark … and now I'm still.

The mist clears, and I'm standing on the edge of a long lake. Beautiful tall pine trees all around. Hills on the other side and high snowcapped mountains in the background.

Drums. I hear the sound of distant drums coming from the other shore a couple of miles or so away.

Now there's movement on the lake. The lake is frozen and a line of people are coming toward me. But not in a straight line—they seem to be weaving their way to me. Very fast. And the drums are getting louder. They're closer now and there are many of them. They're Indians—American Indians! I'm scared, but I see their faces, and they're smiling at me.

I'm standing on the lake, and I'm naked. I look around me and there are others like me, white and naked. We look at each other, puzzled and expectant.

Now we're in a circle, all together with the Native Americans. Their faces are so open and inviting. And happy.

We're dancing, all of us, naked on the surface of the lake. The drums are all through us and the movements come easily and naturally, as though we've always known them. No words are spoken, and we dance for hours. Sweating, breathing, beating. It's magnificent! As we look around the circle, we laugh: we know each other—we touch each other's souls.

There's really nothing more to add to that, other than it was probably the best I've ever felt in my life—in this life—as I was totally conscious at the time and was starting to come to the realization that these alternate realities perhaps needn't be separated from our own. They may in fact, be all layers of the same onion.

The Native American aspect of the experience fascinated me, as I'd never felt any particular affiliation to that culture or its ways. It was true that I did see native cultures as generally superior to our own; I've long felt that we've lost our way to materialism. But that's a feeling I've always had within me, not a doctrine or fanaticism. I remember the first time I was in Indonesia, seeing many of the villagers smiling, their open faces a pickax to my Western guardedness. They seemed to be genuinely happy. Something in me shattered then, for the better. And no words were spoken. Real smiles ... open faces.

And so it had the feeling of an initiation of sorts. But to what, or *from* what? Once again, I couldn't shake off the fascination with the mechanics of the whole thing. Who or what was guiding me to and through these experiences? And if these experiences were shaping who I was, where I was going, and what I was doing with my life, then how much control over my life—or my destiny—did I really have? Was I a puppet? Were we all puppets with our strings being shortened this way or lengthened that way while we slept? The inklings we'd get, to go this way or choose that path: were they *our* inklings? Or did they come from a higher source? An "adjustment bureau" of a kind, perhaps?

Whatever it was, whoever they were— a higher aspect of ourselves or a heavenly band of particularly clever and well-connected puppet masters, or both—I began to sense a deep and unshakeable trust emerging from the space between the constructs of my intellect and my belief system. You see, little by little, those were being edged out of the game. And they were being replaced with something that was way beyond their grasp.

CHAPTER 8

Who's Who?

Lucid (adjective): expressed
clearly; easy to understand.
Psychology (of a dream) experienced with the
dreamer feeling awake,
aware of dreaming, and able to
control events consciously.
Origin: late 16 century: from Latin
lucidus from *lucere* 'shine,'
from *lux*, *luc-* 'light.'—*Oxford Dictionaries*

It was time to truly test things, to man up a bit. This—whatever it was—was potentially a great tool. If my translucent, quasi-invisible, metallic-sounding, ankle-holding, flying crystal man could take me anywhere, to any dimension, to any world, perhaps he could take me to any time, past or future? I began to plan my assault and lay in wait for the prime moment.

And it came sooner than later. While hovering in the phase between being lifted out of my body and being whisked away to be shown something, I mentally placed the intention: *I want to see my death.*

> I'm lying on a beige carpet looking up at the ceiling. I can't seem to get up. I don't recognize the room. There's a large floor to ceiling window in front of me; to the right, a door. It feels like a hotel room. There's a made-up bed a few feet from my head. I want to reach out to it, but I don't have the strength. Next to my head the floor is red. It's blood, and I'm drowning in it. My temples are pounding and my heart is in my throat. No energy even to choke. I'm stuck. Don't panic, don't panic, don't panic, let go ... let go ...

What was remarkable was that when I gained normal waking consciousness again, none of the physiological symptoms remained with me, not even for a second. I went from a body in full panic mode with palpitating heart and fighting for breath, to immediate and absolute calm. Although the experience was completely real, I was left wondering whether I had been shown this lifetime's endpoint or merely me ... *dying*, as in an actor portraying the act of dying. I may yet find out more on this subject, but one thing is for sure: I'll know that room if I ever see it again.

✳ ✳ ✳

The drowning sensation put me in mind of a particularly lucid dream I'd had many years before while enduring adolescence. The dream was a culmination of a spate of such lucid dreams where I was fully conscious of the fact that I was dreaming, and more or less able to determine the general direction of the dream's content. The dreams preceding it were fueled by teenage anger and sexual frustration and would follow the same basic scenario: I would be walking along a manufactured street, manufacture a house to one side, and enter the house to find a manufactured woman I would coerce into having sex with me. It generally ended with the woman somehow falling apart during the act or flatly refusing to cooperate, which I found strange as she was my creation. I remember occasionally marveling at this phenomenon of conjuring up anything I wanted to and once spirited up a chocolate ice-cream cone. It tasted great and so realistic, yet I had no idea of the recipe. That confounded me.

And so to the final, vivid lucid dream that would end in terror. I was walking alone along a bush track when in front of me I saw an old man and a young boy sitting and fishing together on the bank of a deep and fast-flowing river. It was a beautifully peaceful scene, and as I snuck up quietly behind them, the energy between them spoke of a loving grandfather/grandson relationship. With a palm placed on each back and with great exertion, I managed to push them both into the river. I, however, lost my balance in the process and unwittingly followed them into the water, which was surprisingly wet—and cold. And I fell deeper. And the water was all around me. My eyes were open underwater as I kicked and struggled to get to the surface. But I couldn't. My lungs started to fill with water, and I wanted to wake up now. It was my dream! But I continued to sink and take in water, and my lungs were really hurting. I was drowning.

And that was the last in a line of such lucid dreams until the astral wind began to blow my way over twenty years later. I always had the feeling that I'd somehow upset someone or something with my actions; that I'd betrayed an unwritten code of lucid dreamworld ethics and was therefore denied the ability to dream further in that state. Why would I be punished for drowning two of my own creations? Were these entities, in fact, solely my creation? Or were they something else … were they messengers of a sort to help me kill an ego within me? Did an aspect of their essence exist in their own right? You see, this is what I mean about life *not* being a test, as some would argue, but instead a *service:* a guide to greater fulfillment as a being. After these experiences, I was to be far more respectful of dream dwellers, and I've learned in the astral to be particularly genuine when relating to its inhabitants.

One classic example found me dreaming lucidly in a large cave with no one around except for a few boulders. As I looked around for something to catch my eye, I noticed one by the entrance to be particularly 3-D—or animated—in nature.

Focusing all my attention in on it, I feel the wind rush in my ears and forehead as I am pulled into an astral dimension. The cave becomes real, and where the rock had once been stands a youngish man in a rather dapper-looking dark suit. A few others are milling around the cave as would tourists at an attraction.

In these "social" situations, I'm always relieved to find myself dressed as distinct from naked, which is so often the case when I happen upon lonely planets or unpopulated regions. My first thought is "Who dressed me?" followed immediately by "I've never seen these clothes before, but they look fine." And the clothing is always appropriate to the scene. Clever strings being pulled, indeed.

Also, a quick word of warning: if you look at yourself, as in your hands or feet, for too long, they will start to disintegrate—from the tips down. They'll just kind of *melt*. And you'll soon find yourself back on good old terra firma in the present. It seems to be one of the rules of the astral. I think it may send the message back to your physical body that you want to return and that you're missing your lovely earthborn shell. Advice: focus on what is around you, not your corporeal state.

And so the man in the suit approaches me. As we exchange greetings, I note that he is wearing a badge of a particular religious order that I know to be very involved in the training of astral travel (in the interests of privacy, I would prefer not to mention the organization by name). He tells me he is one of my guides, and I ask him if he indeed belongs to that organization. He says yes, which baffles me for only a moment, because in the next instant we are approached by a woman I recognize. She says to the man, "No, you're not his guide—I am," to which the immaculately groomed chap reconsiders his position, politely concedes, and walks away.

I do recognize the woman as a guide. She was in that first bizarre encounter in the medieval Welsh inn—and interestingly enough, she'd actually aged and now seemed to be into her fifties. I've heard her voice many times since, in the astral state, in the manner of training and advice. More of that later in the book.

I leave the cave with my guide to find quite a few people outside, seemingly waiting for something. There's an edginess in the air. A woman shoves her way to the front, visibly upset and emotional. She grabs my arm and tells me that I must help her; that she was murdered by her husband and that I must help her bring him to justice. I'm shocked. I look to my guide, who's standing by me stony-faced. I apologize to the woman and tell her I can't help. She seems destitute. I look at the others standing around waiting, and I can't do it—I really don't want to do it. It's too upsetting, and I leave.

Okay. So have I let them down? Was that my destiny? I couldn't do it. I had the overwhelming feeling not to meddle. Where would it end? In hindsight, I might have been a bit of a wimp and may choose to go back there one day. But you see, as strange as it sounds in this context, I was actually a little afraid of ghosts—and was scared. And to be honest, I sometimes still have problems closing my eyes at night, because I never know just what might pop up in front of me as soon as I do. I know it's something that I have to come to terms with if I really wish to be the master of my energies, and it has its roots in an experience I had in my late twenties (around ten years before my my astral awakening), when I was staying in an old house on the coast in country Australia.

Strange. A purple mist, like sparkles streaming from a sparkler, at the end of the bed. But this is obviously a dream, even though the room appears precisely as it normally would, apart from a bust of Beethoven on the dresser, which wouldn't normally be there.

Greg, speaks the mist in a very kindly, older man's voice, *would you like to make contact with Slim?* (Slim was an old school friend who had recently died.)

Oh shit … it speaks! But it's just a dream; it's okay.

"Ah yeah, sure." If it's a dream, why am I shaking?

Close your eyes and imagine you're holding his hand. Then you will feel him. After a pause, the voice asked, *Do you feel him?*

"Ahh … yep!" (I didn't).

No you don't.

Isn't this my dream?

Concentrate. Think of Slim.

And then I felt it. I felt fingers interlock with my right hand. Invisible spirit fingers, so real—and carrying the essence of Slim. Boy, did I let out a scream. Sheer primal fear!

My girlfriend at the time, who was sharing a bed with me, jumped so high she almost didn't make the bed on the way down. Upon awaking, I found myself sitting up in exactly the same position as I had been throughout the entire dream—if that's what you would call it. For the next eighteen months, I was on sleeping tablets and would only sleep with the lights on, with my head under the blankets (which makes it very difficult to breathe, as many of you could no doubt attest).

That experience, which followed on the heels of us both hearing our recently departed, beloved cat meow from the back of the car while we were doing 150 km/h on an old dirt back road (when you would normally hear *nothing*) led me to the startling realization that the *beyond* may be merely a shadow away—especially, it would

75

seem, in certain places. Okay, the cat I had been close to. Perhaps there had been some emotional connection or desire. But the fact that both my girlfriend and I heard it at exactly the same time and had swung our heads around in tandem at a crystal-clear meow—*his* meow—coming from an empty back seat was compelling. And Slim ... to be honest, I didn't really know him that well. He hadn't been that close a friend. Once again, I can't shake off the feeling that guidance is involved here. A shaping or a gentle nudging in the direction of a belief or an interest. Or a preparation. And with time, these things have a way of incubating, until a moment that is deemed appropriate comes along.

These days, I sense ghosts or spirits wandering around, ostensibly invisibly in our dimensions, as a not unpleasant skin-crawling sensation, a little similar to goose bumps. Sometimes I'll hear their sighs or smell an unusual scent. And I'm okay with it. Generally, they are there for a reason, and I'll have a chat with them. There are many of them in the astral realms; usually those who have recently passed and still have unfinished business to attend to (or think that they have) and those who won't move on for whatever reason. If you feel they're around and you don't wish to be bothered by them, just show them a little empathy and let them know your wishes.

In the end, it's really not so strange.

CHAPTER 9

Moonlighting

It is a classic, quaint, ye olde English shoppe. As I push open the wooden door, a little bell tinkles above. Inside all is cozy, warm, and very quiet, with a welcoming smell of sweetness and dust. So much detail. The shelves are laden with canisters bearing labels I can't read. Strange-shaped sweets or biscuits are piled into small and colorful trays on the worn wooden counter. A woman is serving and two customers, a man and a woman, are standing in front of me. They seem slightly uncomfortable at my presence.

M any places I've visited are like carbon copies of our own Earth cities but with slight differences. I once approached a woman on a very busy English-looking city street and asked her where I was.

"London … where else?" she answered in a bemused tone.

"I mean, what country are we in?"

"London, as I just said." Now she was becoming irritated.

"And the city is?"

"England, of course!"

"So, we're in England, which is in London?"

"*Yes!*" she snapped, at which point she angrily and suspiciously turned on her heel.

As I stood on that busy street with the world flying past me and hundreds of people going about their lives, I marveled at the detail of all that was on display. The buildings were just like London but not quite the same. The smell of the place, the traffic, the vibe … something felt different. But the people could see me—that was interesting. And that wasn't always the case. When I felt I was on the Earth, in this reality but in another dimension, most people couldn't see me or communicate with me.

Often in these situations, I would freak out and try to get as much information on the place as I could. In this particular Londonesque world, I remember running to the closest street sign only to find it written in such gobbledygook that I became utterly panicked in trying to commit the name to memory. The letters were the same as ours, but the words were so long and convoluted. Often when I would try to read something like a newspaper or a book, the words would make sense at first and then, literally, start to swim in front of my eyes. Not always but often. I felt it was a bit like looking at the hands or focusing too much on a particular detail—things would just start to fall apart. Unless there was a specific message for me, written words just weren't going to stay sober.

In one adventure, I was walking around what felt like a North American city, with everything seeming a little retro. Nobody seemed to notice me, and so I went about one of my favorite pastimes of walking through people or, more correctly, standing still while they walked through me. I could actually *feel* them as they passed through; it was a slight resistance of sorts. And I could sense their particular drama or state of mind immediately. And some seemed to notice it. A very slight hesitation in their step. Could they sense me? Was I somehow interacting with them, and could I influence them in some way? Should I be doing so? I spotted a corner newsstand and feverishly half-flew toward it. You sometimes have to watch the whole flying thing: you can take off so fast that that you simply exit the dimension. I've often found it better to fly very low to keep in touch with the landscape or—over short distances—focus in on the intended target and mentally urge yourself to be there. When you do this, you actually experience the spatial movement between yourself and the object without seeming to lose your uprightness. That's what I term *half-flying*. I was able to pick up a newspaper—or what I believe to be the *energy* of the paper—and quickly scan for a date. The year was 1960, clear as day, and the print seemed to match. Then it all started to swim (I've really got to find a way of alleviating that problem). I think I got overexcited, as I was immediately zapped back into my sleeping body. One really has to try to reign in one's emotions in the astral, otherwise the body tends to unceremoniously yank you back. I believe that to be a in-built survival mechanism.

Real people, with real minds in a real dimension. Just *other* than ours.

Sometimes I would just astrally pop out in the atmosphere of an Earth city. On one such occasion, I found myself viewing a modern cityscape from around two hundred feet above the ground. I didn't seem to have any body at all: just a perfect, non-adjustable, 180-degree view directly in front of me. I felt like a probe. Directly behind the city was a range of high snow-capped mountains. The scene was absolutely clear and in ultra-high definition. I immediately went to work memorizing structures and landmarks for later research. And I also had a feeling: *Canada*. It didn't take me long to find out, thanks to computer images, that it had been Vancouver. It was a perfect match. But what was the relevance? Why had I been shown this?

This particular phenomenon was happening a lot before I had the energy chip removed from my forehead. Funnily enough, I often had the sensation that someone else was seeing through my eyes during these times. What if the laser treatment had been an operation to place a kind of camera in my forehead for others to see what I see? I would often remark to Moni that I felt someone else was looking through me, and this did stop—this particular feeling—after I'd seen the Reiki master and had the chip removed. Was I moonlighting as an alien probe? Pictures, emotions, scenes ... what better way to learn about such volatile beings as ourselves? I'm partly joking here but partly not. In fact, for the most part, *not*. For what I've experienced truly is stranger than fiction.

*　*　*

Getting back to the energetic aspect of things. I ask you again: What *isn't* energy? When we watch a movie, our energy absorbs the storyline, the setting, the characters; we connect with what's happening on a far more visceral level than a purely intellectual one. And if the acting is particularly authentic, our emotions actually sync with the characters. In fact, that is the role of an actor—to match our vibration with theirs. And this process occurs absolutely naturally and effortlessly. It's called *projection*. You see, the body is essentially (and when I say body, I'm referring to all our bodies, including the mind) a transmitter; we are sending and receiving signals continuously. It's all a play of energy. I ask you once again to turn inward, close your eyes, and feel the buzz. That's your true body; that's the one that contains your physical body—not the other way around. That is, in fact, the template of your flesh-and-blood body. It exists always and in constant perfection. And because it precedes the physical, all illness or injury will be felt here before it enters the physical.

Tapping in to this ostensibly invisible resource can bring about remarkable healing and rejuvenation as well as activating the preemptive and predictive within us. It tells us when things are going awry, or not, beforehand, and in so doing, gives us a choice of how to continue. It contains no emotion, as it is perfection—way above the emotional state—and is beyond the capacity or need to judge. For emotions are choices. Do you really think that happy means jumping up and down in hysterics when something good happens to you? I put it to you that *happy* is the natural state of being. It's who we truly are, and this invisible body of ours is a key to recovering it. And it's certainly not about being a zombie when all the world is in a fit. Far from it. It's about being authentic, real, and powerful.

Ah, a rant! Yes, but a good one, and it felt mighty good at that! Try it. Try being less reactive at both ends of the scale and see how you feel. You might just like it.

* * *

And so, the alien probe thing. Not so outlandish to me. Rather like a stage actor, I may have been a conductor of human experience, one angle of the saga. When I would project my energy out into space to connect with this particular intelligence, Moni would always sense the shift within the house. Things became a little weird. There was a definite presence in the house, and it was often, as I mentioned earlier, somehow scary. But I did learn a lot about projecting a signal out into the ether. Firing up the astral, inner body with a purpose or request was the key to its activation and transmission. Holding a clear desire or question within this buzzing life-force and mentally expanding your energy field to let the intention fly—it's a very powerful process, and like anything, it gets easier the more you do it. As a trained musician, I would always marvel at how the body would find its own way to make things easier or better. Improvement is seemingly built into the human hard drive. So it is with astral projection. You've just got to give it a bit of a shake to get it—*you*—to wake up and get happening.

Really, what you are doing in tuning in to this process is expanding your sensitivity or level of awareness. Many years ago— long before that initial tunnel experience—I was visiting my brother, who was living in Montana at the time. Hanging on the wall of the bedroom where I was sleeping was an old American Indian hand drum. I paid it no attention at the time—in fact, I never really noticed it as I fell asleep that first night. But it noticed me. As I was losing consciousness and on the threshold of sleep, I saw the face of an Indian watching me from the drum. Needless to say, it freaked me out, and I had the drum promptly removed from the room. And there is a distinction between an active imagination and *something else*. This is something you just *know*. My brother was later to find out that the drum was indeed an authentic antique and had belonged to a medicine man. The drum was imbued with his energy, and as energy always *is,* the drum—and in effect his spirit within the drum—will always live on. Who knows what he may have shared with me if I had remained calm. I can just see one of those posters: Keep Calm … When You Open Your Astral Eyes!

But can you see my point about being less reactive and rethinking your automatic response system? What are we really afraid of when we expand our consciousness? Being burned at the stake perhaps? Who knows what traumas were inflicted in our past lives (for we do have them, you know—all of us) for being able to see beyond the mere physical. And remnants of these traumas are still within us, like shards of glass, freezing us unwittingly into our shackles. Much effort has been expended over the past age by religious dogma and social mores to keep us imprisoned, in a way, in the material world. Fear has become the ruling premise. Fear of the unknown, fear of attack, fear of going mad, fear of losing your job, fear of the devil, fear of losing your house, and of course, the worst of them all, the Big Kahuna no less—fear of an economic crisis (said, of course, in a deep, booming, reverberating voice). Our stuff ... our beloved stuff! ... may lose its value! What about our real stuff: who and what *we* are? Isn't that more important to discover? Perhaps the distraction of our age away from the recognition of innate human happiness serves to line the pockets and feed the egos of a certain few—a massive understatement, I know—but do we really want to keep going along with and supporting that?

Releasing fear and opening up the mind will assist you in reaching this stillness that seems to enliven the astral body, your truer self. Your awareness will begin to unfold and expand to experience the greater reality and universal consciousness—and in so doing, your need to fear will subside. And from there, it's a self-perpetuating engine, in that you'll only get clearer and clearer, and feel freer and happier—as in genuinely and consistently more content. And that is the true human condition.

CHAPTER 10

The True Color
of Christmas

I'm with them here again, around the table. They're leaning in toward me and listening very carefully, their eyes transfixed into mine. They seem concerned with what I'm saying, yet my words sound distant and emanate from somewhere else altogether. I can't get over their faces, so clear and unlined, and their eyes so open. They tell me to be patient and that one day I will come home. I feel good here.

One of the most interesting methods of astral transportation is the elevator. I've involuntarily experienced this on several occasions and found it to be quite ... I was going to say *uplifting,* but as I wish you to take me seriously, I'll say *pleasant.*

I'm awake, and my body is shifting. Now I'm vertical, but I still can't see. Okay, I'm going up—slowly. It's like I hear machinery. Now I've stopped. A narrow, horizontal grate opens up in the darkness a couple of feet in front of my face. I see two eyes looking at me. Closed, and up I go. The same speed, just like an elevator. Again, another grate, more eyes— more than two. Closed, and up I go again. I'm being checked out. Energetically. That's what I feel. Open, closed, up. The pattern repeats. The grates are slightly different in shape each time, as are the eyes and their number.

Eventually the doors open. It was an elevator! The scene before me is simply lovely. A beautiful, hazy blue sky and trees full of new spring growth. The grass is so green and the colors are ultra-vivid. There are tables all around with people sitting at them, reminiscent of a welcoming outdoor European café on a glorious, warm spring day. As I stroll around the tables, the people seem quite normal—very happy, in fact—as they joke and chat with one another while drinking coffee and tea and eating tasty-looking morsels. Quite bizarre!

The paving under my feet, the scent in the air, the play of light and shade from the trees, the people, the tables … it's all so real. No—it's hyper-real, plunging what would normally constitute the mundane into the realm of the magnificent.

After a time of simply soaking it all in, I politely approach a woman sitting at a table and ask her where we are. She smiles back at me and says, "Heaven." Right. Funny. Very funny.

I must admit: it was a beautiful place. I felt very, very well there. The psychoanalyst would say (in a certain European accent): "Yes, in your mind, you were looking for a refuge, and the café represented …" Fair enough. Although I don't drink coffee. Maybe the tea.

It purely was what it was: a real place, regardless of the connotations of the woman's answer (but who knows?). Once again, the machinations of the whole experience were the things that fascinated me most. Going astral, then into the elevator, and then the eyes scanning me. Part of me thought, *Bugger you! Who are you to judge my access level?* I didn't appreciate being filtered in this way by a team of faceless angelic bouncers, but I guess hierarchies exist in all realms or schemes of things—or so it would seem. You're at where you're at! No more or less. Hmm … perhaps an herbal tea.

The elevators led me to interesting places where I'd often meet with people and certain issues would be discussed. I found their concepts difficult to grasp. They were human in form—both male and female—but seemingly not of Earth. They appeared to have neither egos nor airs and graces, were utterly focused and listened most intently to what I had to say. I would find myself very calmly and lucidly telling them about our situation here on Earth while at the same time wondering where on (can't say that, now can I?) they were from. It would often surprise me what came out of my mouth or mind. It seemed the lack of transparency in our system and the unequal distribution of our resources were linked to our feeling of separation on both inner and outer levels. This was one memorable theme that was discussed at length. We always sat tightly around a rectangular table, with me at one end, in an otherwise empty room. Looking back after each experience, I could never recall hearing their voices. In fact, I don't think we ever actually spoke. Their demeanor was always very serious, yet empathetic and caring. And their eyes seemed so clear—almost too clear. They seemed to have none of the barriers around their faces that we carry. You could actually look into their eyes directly when you engaged them, and I believe that's how we communicated. More and more, I see the human ego as a barrier. We simply don't need it, not at all. It clouds us, is ensconced in fear, and thrives on emotional drama. Contrary to popular belief, we don't need it to survive. Quite the opposite, in fact.

✳   ✳   ✳

Occasionally, I would exit in real-time and come across some rather unusual anomalies.

Okay, my eyes are awake, but my body's asleep, I think. I roll from side to side to loosen the body. Little by little I increase the roll until I'm out of the bed and standing next to it. There we are, my wife and I, lying in bed, apparently asleep. I walk toward the window wall and jump straight through it down into the backyard a level below. Strange. The outer house wall is exactly as it should be, but when I face what should be our smallish garden, there's a large baseball diamond in its place. Nothing moving in the dark. So still. And this baseball field …

Now at this stage, I was becoming most interested in Reiki, and I decided to test a theory. One of the first symbols you learn, in this healing art, is the power symbol, which is a triple spiral bisected by a vertical line. To use these symbols, you draw them in the air with your hand. When you are attuned to Reiki, the symbols are activated in your energy field.

I decide to draw the power symbol to see if anything happens. I'm looking down, as it's an Earth symbol and I assume that if something does show, it will more likely be in that direction. As soon as I draw it, the atmosphere lights up and the symbol is ignited by countless streams of light from above. As I throw my head up I see that the source of this light is the stars. I literally see them streaming the light down to the symbol. The burst soon subsides and I'm left there standing in the dark, on the baseball diamond next to the back of my house, in awe.

This wasn't something I'd anticipated. To be honest, I hadn't anticipated anything. But it was further verification to me of the energetic volatility of the astral dimensions. Here, in the astral, you could *see* energy; you could witness its presence, its power. It wasn't just theory, it was real. And these were old symbols imbued with lifetimes of energy and intent. I later read that Reiki was a gift to us from the stars. Interesting. Also, when you think of the significance of the spiral in so many shamanic traditions … As a realist and a natural skeptic (yes, even after all this had happened to me), I was truly beginning to comprehend the reality of the interaction we have with the universe.

The relevance of the baseball field? Hmm … no idea. It was just there. These anomalies occur constantly when you're in real-time astral. That was a big alteration, but normally they're quite subtle, like door handles missing (I guess you don't need them anyway), pictures and photos changing their content, personal objects changing form or position slightly, and of course, words all a-swim. It's all interesting stuff, and it is tempting to obsess over this phenomenon (I know, because I have), but you can get so lost in the nitty-gritty that you miss the greater picture altogether. I'm convinced we're being guided through these experiences, and they are vehicles of expansion. If you really need to be able to read all the words, you will.

I'm out. Don't think—just see what happens.

Spider webs! (Happens quite a bit, actually.) That's okay, just brush them out of the way. There's something like a low tunnel I have to crawl through on my hands and knees. A bit uncomfortable, but it's not dark. Now there's a mangy ginger cat just a few feet ahead, arching its back and hissing at me. I swipe it to the left and it's gone, revealing a small, arched wooden door at the end of the tunnel. I push it open.

The tunnel opens out into a room. I can see it ahead of me. I pull myself into the room, which is full of colorful, wrapped-up toys. And there's a life-size Santa doll, complete with a pair of big plastic floating eyes, propped up against the wall. Except he's all in green, with brown hair and beard. Hmm.

As I approach him, his head turns to face me. The eyes do their quivering thing. I'm fascinated by this real, totally animated, life-size green Santa doll. I really look into his eyes at close range to see what's there. But they're just toy eyes, dancing every time he moves his head. He meets my gaze and seems somehow embarrassed by my close scrutiny, beckoning with his eyes that I should take something from a box that he is now offering me.

Inside the box is a small folded piece of paper. I open it and see words written in old-fashioned Christmas-style calligraphy. The letters are beautifully ornate and clear. I look up at Santa, who's urging me to read the text, which I do: "Open your heart to the magic of giving." I read it a few times to remember it and see if it will swim away. It doesn't.

Years later, I was to find out that indeed Santa's original suit color was green. Apparently he went to work for Coca Cola in the early 1930s, and had to step up to their corporate image. I think we all did.

His reality of plastic-ness fascinated me in the experience—those so-3-D toy eyes. You really have to experience these things to believe them. And don't just take my word for it, try getting out for yourself. If this book can only serve to give you the slightest of nudges in the general direction of the possibility of experiencing the astral dimensions, then I've done what I set out do.

The message he delivered was as clear as clear can be. Literally. It didn't run away. And that's what I mean about the guided aspect of it all: the words were meant to be read, by me. The whole reality was couched in such an exciting, naïve setting. There was a purity to it; it was filled with the delight of childhood and innocent joy, including the fact that Santa was dressed in his original color, green, as distinct from the purely commercial connotation that his modern-day souped-up image tends to evoke in us. The sentiment it conjured up in me was, in a way, *magical*. It's hard to explain, but it's about more than just receiving a message. It's about the penny dropping exactly when and where it should and the reverberations that come with it. And it did affect me. At that time in my life I was teaching and often felt underwhelmed by the performance of my students. I let that feeling define me for a time. Then I started to connect purely for teaching's sake, not for the expectation of a result. I started to give of myself as a person without the need for any reward, and boy, did the world open up! I had so much more energy at work, and I began to genuinely enjoy my students. The results would look after themselves, which they did. And that was just at work. Personally, I felt a greater sense of surrender to the interplay of life. I lost the need to control my situation and allowed my heart more rein. I let go.

I could feel the reactive urge within me sizzling out that little bit further. It was losing its wax and, in so doing, freeing me just that little bit more ... *to be.*

CHAPTER 11

Witches and Dragons

Empathy (noun): the ability to understand and
share the feelings of another.
—*Oxford Dictionaries*

N ow it was time for the wars and a little sojourn in the desert.
I had just begun my two-year, final-level course training to
be a Reiki master, and I was having a chat with someone who'd just
finished the level herself. She asked me in a concerned tone how I
was feeling, as she had just been to hell and back. "Fine, absolutely
great!" I told her. Just as I said it, I became acutely aware of the sound
of water trickling from the fountain in the front yard. All I could
hear was the water. It got louder and louder and was soon roaring
through my ears. And it carried such bleakness, such weight.

That night, I had a strange dream. In it, a man spoke to me:
"Greg, you are experiencing evanescence, the same separation that

Christ experienced before his union. It is important and necessary that you go through this."

But I'm not religious! And just what is *evanescence?* Apparently it means evaporating, dissolving, vanishing—what a fascinating word to use. And this whole religious thing? Geez! (I didn't say Jesus). I don't get it. Things were going so well.

Needless to say, it truly was an appalling time. At this stage, I didn't have the little Buddha within me laughing his belly raw at the most inappropriate of times—he was to come later. But another banishment from whatever I was being banished from? And this time, it sounded serious: the man's voice sounded a little too empathic. I had been enjoying feeling the Reiki flow; I'd been enjoying a particularly clear and peaceful mind when I meditated. Everything around me seemed to have a real sparkle, and I very rarely felt disconnected or depressed. But no, not now.

Not only did everything get heavy and particularly trudge-like, but the things I normally enjoyed just didn't seem to cut it. Surfing just wasn't popping the plastic bag around my head as it normally did. Reiki, TV, food … oh yeah, *whatever!* Forget meditating—my mind just wasn't my own, or that's how it felt. But it wasn't just the lack of luster that was getting me down, I became very dark. In fact, intensely so. And that was when the wars began.

I'm out of my body and into nothingness. Something feels strange. My shoulder—I've been hit! I swing around in midair, and there she is. WTF? A witch? And she's hurling balls of energy at me! I duck a few, but generally, I'm getting hammered. I feel my energy body depleting with each blow. What is this? And she's as real as day. I'm seriously scared.

Oh, and this was just to be the beginning of my clash with the evil powers, the dark side, the witches and the warlocks—whatever you want to call it/them. But why? I'd learned well to protect myself. I knew that it was an energy minefield out there, both here and in other dimensions, and I had copious methods with which to deal with the negative: light, symbols, incantations, swear words. Why the challenge? Why me? And most of all, why had I been abandoned?

The clashes in *this* reality seemed to escalate too. They had real power over me. My solar plexus was in overdrive around certain people, and I couldn't seem to maintain my equilibrium. Nowhere near it. And so I had a few run-ins. Yeah, I lost it a bit! The grace I'd been feeling, the empathy, the lack of reactivity had dissolved between my toes like quicksilver. Moreover, the sense of calm I'd spent years building had been replaced by stress, that most dangerous and carcinogenic entity.

Plus, I had the hands yanking me out of my body at night— not always the coziest of feelings—plunging me into *Buffy*-style encounters of the ugliest kind. I'd never even watched such shows, *so why was I in them?* I knew I had to face this head-on, and not to go out would have been stalling the inevitable. So there I was, screaming abuse at her ugliness and most evilness (she actually did look very scary, I have to say) and getting absolutely nowhere. Why was she refusing to leave my field?

* * *

The dark: just what is it? I remember very early in my astral career encountering it for the first time. We were staying overnight at a friend's house in a small Austrian village. Everything seemed fine going to bed: there didn't seem to be any weird vibe in the room or the house. Just as I fell asleep, it came. Having done the exercises to fall asleep as consciously as I could and just before that seductive slide into the never-never, the dark shouldered its way into my field, stage left. Like a block outline of the upper body of a man's silhouette, it edged its way further and further into my field. I'd open my eyes, shake it off, close them again, and there it was again, in full eclipse mode. Now this was frightening, because *I knew it was there* and its energy left me in frozen, stricken fear. What was it all about? Was I being checked out in some way by this energy?

There is much fear banked up in the astral dimensions, particularly in the lower ones—as was mentioned earlier—that are closer in proximity and vibration to our own 3-D physical world. Entities are literally birthed into creation by the collective human fear, as humans through their suffering give off or experience feelings of despair, hopelessness, and anger. Multiply that by generations, and you infect what should be a template of joy and light and limitlessness—the lower astral dimensions—with a continuum of negative energy. This, in turn, powers the collective human ego (ego equals fear, by the way), which needn't and shouldn't actually exist and which, in its turn, keeps the karmic wheel of our reincarnation in this dimension turning and turning, over and over again, rather like a water wheel churning through the same old water for eons. We need to change the water; it's gotten a little stinky!

You've been to places, cities, where terrible human tragedies have occurred. Have you ever sensed the energy there? Have you ever felt sad or strangely uncomfortable in these places? Just as positive or light places carry positive energy, so do places of trauma carry the opposite. It's actually simple science and very, very real. I know because I can see it, as you can see your hand, and I can feel it, as you can feel the warmth of the sun on your face. Tuning into this field and acknowledging its existence is the first step we can take in healing ourselves as a species. The second step is to be less reactive to so-called negative situations. "Stop feeding the dragon!" should be a sign attached to the Earth's ether. Are you truly prepared to give up the glee of being hard-done by, of being a victim? And there are other things you can do to alleviate the shadow that permeates our template—our astral—our being—as I was soon to discover.

* * *

The battle with this dark power went on for some time. Why it presented itself to me generally in the guise of a woman, I don't know, but I do know that she was pure evil. My efforts to summon up legions of light before I fell asleep just weren't working. And remember, I'd been abandoned in the desert and was way out of Wi-Fi range. It had become a Groundhog Day of sorts, with me clocking up some serious training hours in astral weaponry. What I felt was unfair was that when I would duck, so would her handfuls of burning energy that were being flung at me. And they hurt … *they really hurt!* I sometimes tried remaining calm and non-reactive (as much as I could in the circumstances), but she'd stare me down, her eyes so dark and piercing. With her hair streaming off behind her, she gave off a stench that made my bile creep.

Should I go and see someone? Do I need help? Am I going mad? Something inside told me that I had to handle this alone. A test? Or an experience? You judge.

Throughout these duels, we never spoke, as I'd long ago given up abusing her verbally. I did develop a method of swirling up my own energy and firing it to intercept her pain-balls just before they hit me, although I don't think I ever made a direct hit on her. I became quite adept at this form of protection if I stayed especially focused, and I surprised myself on one particular occasion by my speed of movement and precision hurling. It was in the midst of this exchange that she spoke to me for the first time.

"You're getting quite good at that, aren't you? The whole defending thing."

A compliment? And then she was right by me, her face a foot from mine. So utterly frightening and disgusting. Yet—there was *something*. For some inexplicable reason and for the tiniest fragment of a moment, my heart softened, and I felt a kind of empathy for her. At that instant, her face transformed into one of absolute beauty and radiance, and she shone such a smile at me and said, "You see, Greg, it's all the same."

And in that moment, I knew that there was no such thing as evil or fear; that it was a part of love, that it was a choice, a miscomprehension, a misinterpretation. There was nothing to fear, as it didn't actually exist. It was merely the face of light seen through our own shadow. And even that shadow didn't exist. Empathy, just a little empathy.

How the Earth would change if we could all just let out a deep breath and let ourselves off the hook; if we could bring that smile into our interior and let it take seed where the arid and parched lie unattended, untouched. What a true paradise we'd have! And it all starts with the individual. You are the center of the universe, you know—star matter in human form. Don't you see? It's time to flick the switch.

And that spelled the end of my own personal Desert Storm. The victory was in surrender; surrender to the heart. Interestingly enough, as the body's major energy center, the heart is the primary driver responsible for the projection of the astral double. How fitting, don't you think? When you begin to project, it powers the astral engine that enables the splitting process to occur. You'll actually feel it beating very fast, palpitating in fact. But it's nothing to fear, it's just the energy of your heart racing: its *chakra* or energy wheel, as the ancients termed it. You're quite safe—it's loud and intense, but you won't have a heart attack as many profess you might. If your actual heart were beating too quickly, you'd wake up! The process is safe and natural. It's a skill, a sense, that for certain reasons has been bred out of us over generations.

But it's now time to reactivate that sense. Sure, it doesn't necessarily serve the economy as we know it, nor does it foster war—but it does give us, as beings, new eyes to see through the cloud of oppression we've helped to build around ourselves. It's a gateway to the truth that we, as individuals and as a collective, are innately aware of, lurking just beneath the surface.

Chapter 12

Say What?

I'm suspended yet moving at lightning speed through a space that is both dark and vast. An enormous tone is sounded, penetrating all layers of my consciousness and emanating from all directions. For the briefest of moments (that borders on eternity) I am the All; I Am. It's a male voice that is sounding. And it's a very, very low *om*.

Astral sounds, voices, messages: absolutely fascinating stuff. I was once walking in a field in rural Austria—as one is prone to do, for some reason—when I came to a sudden halt. *What was that?* And then I heard it. I recognized the sound from an earlier astral expedition: it was the Music of the Spheres. I looked up and I could distinctly hear the deep, metallic, grinding vibration from the heavens. I don't know how else to describe it, but you could sense physically the great, majestic rotation of the spheres above. Fantastic!

On other occasions, I would hear very deep and all-penetrating tones upon entering the void, particularly in real-time dimensional travel. The time I flew from Munich to Vienna (at a bargain rate) was a prime example. After I'd made my intention clear as to my destination, I found myself hovering but at the same time moving at lightning speed through a dark void of seemingly infinite space. In an all-consuming, booming, deeper than the deepest male basso-profundo voice, the sound of *om* rang out through the void. Magnificent, very real, and quite alarming! It was as though the very consciousness of the universe had put fly to song. Had I not been so interested, I would have been too scared to go on, but it really was a magnificent sound—*vibration*—to behold, to be a part of. How can I justly express to you the absolute clarity, the absolute reality, with which I experienced this? And the sheer wonder of it all.

While I'm not a Buddhist, it was a clear, resounding, unmistakable *om*. So it's not just an arbitrary sound then, is it? It actually exists. And I now know that to be a fact, thanks to astral travel. I don't even feel the need to look it up or Google it (which I haven't), because the knowledge is within me now. It always was, but now I'm conscious of it. Can you see the profound value of such a tool?

A few years after my astral awakening, I began to hear disembodied voices speaking to me occasionally, particularly upon awakening. There were two of them: a kindly male voice and a female voice I recognized as one of my guides. I would most often be addressed by name, and the content of their messages was always of a provocative and deeply personal nature. It's my belief that we all receive these messages from our guides but that we're just not remembering them, as we've fallen into the pattern of being mostly unconscious when we traverse the mystical regions between being asleep and being fully awake.

When I hear these voices, I'm in this reality. I've woken up, but I try to maintain the sense of limitlessness for as long as I can. In this state, of only a few seconds perhaps, your normal physical senses can defy the limitations of time and space as they are effectively suspended between this reality and the greater consciousness. You can receive a message of some length, delivered in a relaxed and normal tempo, in a fraction of a second. You see, your astral senses—or second senses—are not limited to the boundaries of Earth's physical laws (although I do note that modern physics is catching on).

While the voices are heard in the actual ears—along with a slight physical vibration directly behind them—it's as though they enter my head through the very top of the skull. I can actually feel movement in this area of my brain when it happens. I've even heard voices with my physical eyes wide open and the buzz still persisting. Once again, it's a feeling as though a download is occurring. And it's a very pleasant sensation, this inbuilt human Wi-Fi receiver of ours.

The first message I received in this manner was quite cryptic and delivered in the male voice after a particularly vivid dream (not a lucid one) where I watched a woman intentionally allow herself to be set alight and burned: *Greg, what injures more personally than those who are injured?*

Say what? Is that even English? Using the same word derivative twice in the same sentence? Not to mention: who are you?

What injures more personally … what injures more personally … Once I got over my ego and tossed the being-clever world out the window, I began to make whatever mortal sense I could out of it.

First of all, I had just woken up after the dream, which had been quite full-on, and I was musing over it when the voice spoke. I instinctively looked around the room, as the voice had been that clear.

Okay, so I'd been studying this healing method, Reiki, quite intensely, and I had been delving astrally into the nature of disease. Things were becoming clearer to me as to the true nature and cause of many of the illnesses of my clients. But my ego was taking a bashing, big time. As you've gathered, these second senses within me were all astir, and they would often send me clear pictures or scenes during treatments with clients, even feelings, that would relate directly to the problem the client was experiencing. (Interesting that the voice favored the word *injured* over *ill*.) But it wasn't always my call. It's often painful for someone to recover from a trauma so engrained into their person that perhaps it has become a defining characteristic for them. They believe it to *be* them.

And so all these tools I'd been developing—essentially *finding clarity*—remained, often, merely that: tools hanging in the work shed. What was my problem? Why couldn't I accept that some people didn't want to be that clear? Because that's what I believe being well and healthy is: it's being clear. That's not to deny that many people benefited from the treatments I was giving, but I wanted more—*I* wanted to be in control.

I had a feeling, though, that this cryptically delivered message wasn't just about that. There was something else that would take much longer to resolve. You see, like many of us, I felt I wasn't in my tribe—simple words that can cause the heart to ache for a lifetime. I was lucky. I'd found my soul mate, who I'd just married. But the clarity of the astral, the humility, the simplicity, the beauty ... *that was my tribe!* How could I ever feel genuinely content and fit in with this world when I knew there to be other beings and realms of reason … actually, no, beyond reason—of true heart? Was the world that bad, that far gone?

I remember once as a teenager, looking lustfully into the face of a girl in a hard-core pornographic magazine that was being passed around the circle in one of the supposed rites of passage served up to us (at a profit, no less) by the older generation. As every boy knows in our culture, this goes on for a few years (at best) and stirs up feelings of lust, longing, disgust, and above all, confusion. At that fateful moment, as I stared into those drug-addled airbrushed eyes, I suddenly—and without any warning—saw the face of a human being. Frantically scanning the next few pages, convinced of my error, I saw even more human beings. As I later slunk away from the circle, I tried to maintain the eyes of the knowing and the jeering, but I knew deep down that I'd failed the rite.

Ahh, the grim, dark secret of mankind—of our age. It starts to rear its craggy form at school, hiding behind the respectability of the crest, the cap, the uniform. Its sinuous, muscular arms cradle us a little too snugly as we embark on a voyage of desensitization, disinformation, humiliation, and conformity. It throws back its narrow bony head in delight and with a flick of its tongue lets out a mighty, otherworldly bellow of derision and satisfaction as it watches us take our first wobbly steps into the supposed realm of manhood.

Wrong realm.

Love sports, love math, love music … why the pit in the gut? I'm twelve and am still coloring in the three kings. That's divinity? Please explain. *You can't be an archeologist—there are no jobs in that field.* Okay. Why aren't there any girls around? *Because it's a boys' school, and they'll distract you.* Why? *Sex.* What exactly is that? *Ha, ha! We're the teachers, we'll make fun of it; you shut up and keep coloring.* I'm learning, I'm quite popular, I appear to be reasonably clever ... but why the pit? Why the constant pit?

School. Hmm ... Education: whose thoughts, whose purposes? I felt the narrowing, for sure; the hands, firm to the side of the head with the neck straining, *that way ... c'mon ... look that way.* (Unfunnily enough, I was to have real problems with my neck all throughout my education.) The absence of any scope to question. Surely adults could learn something from us as well. And then there was the great dumbing down, the incessant pummeling and grinding of individuality and sensibility into the pulp of hapless mediocrity by the ever-active bully stratum of the student body, who of course thrived in such degenerative conditions. These not-so-bright but apparently very normal students—who would later feed the ranks of the bloated and suited upper-middle class—had the begrudging fear and support of the corresponding bully stratum of staff members, to almost complete the coup. There is something unquestionably dark going on here; something of gargantuan proportions. It's the big *Shhhhhh*! Silent and subtle, and as forceful as a force-eight hurricane.

But what is it really, and what am I actually jabbering on about?

First, let's try a bit of clinical reverse-engineering. (I say *clinical* because I'm not being emotive on the subject, I'm merely pointing it out.) Phenomenally unequal wealth distribution in the world resulting in cataclysmic levels of poverty, sickness, and starvation, yet there are unparalleled levels of education in the world. Peoples, countries, ideologies, religions still at war with one another, yet there are unparalleled levels of education in the world. Global warming and the world's population increasing exponentially as the Earth's resources continue to deplete, yet there are unparalleled levels of education in the world.

And is the measure of a country, a society, a man or woman, a world, really to be figured in terms of economic growth? Is this still a game we're playing? Are we still at school? Whatever happened to the notion of, "When I became a man, I put away childish things"? Surely it's time to leave such petty and childish concepts back in the schoolyard—perhaps bury them under the sandpit (in radioactive-waste-strength disposal bags, cleverly colored in by the year-four class)—and get about the real task of reclaiming our true human sovereignty, acting from a sense of real intelligence and creating a world from a place of heart, compassion, and joy. An adult world, a human world. Isn't that what we should be about? Isn't that what we want?

Those golden, formative years of the human being—such a precious and rare commodity—are being ridiculed, abused, and profited from, for the most part, by preceding generations who act as though they know no better. Who are they who underrate sex and relationships so, who feed us plastic food, who make house prices unaffordable, who tell us the wrong stories, and who don't look us in the eye?

I see so many grey and genuinely unhappy people, marching toylike in their suits as though their deliberate stride will infuse purpose into those grey and lifeless threads. But there's nothing deliberate. Their faces are so wracked with the weight of mock importance and lost soul, and their eyes are so shot with the banal. A childhood stolen, raped, and exploited. They're still at school, traversing the locker-filled corridors like ghosts who don't realize they're dead and that the final bell rang long ago. They're being good, taking it for the team, and speaking in such a babble that their words don't seem to stick anywhere. If only one could dissolve the aspects of education within them that have strangled their concept of humanity with such life-disaffirming notions as limit, lack, and profit margins.

Perhaps, this is the *truer* alien—the one that is so unceremoniously monster-fied by our film industry—all serpentine and feeding itself down the throat of its human victims in such violence and rape, serving not only to propel the myth of the victim of entrapped humanity but at the same time repelling us to any scent of the notion of the friendly galactic visitor. (See? even those words sound absurd.)

So back to the question: who are they who tell us the wrong stories and not look us in the eye? Of course, there's only one answer: fear—the blood of greed, separation, and all things unreal, the bane of our reality that has been drip-feeding the lower astral planes and contaminating the human energy template for eons.

Now I'm not saying this in an echoing, reverberating, major-film-company-release kind of voice (even though it would have sounded good), I'm merely stating it in a matter-of-fact, sitting-at-my-desk-in-Ugg-boots typeface. You see, it's all an illusion; we've been feeding an illusion. That first day you enter institutionalized society, all a-creased and hair parted ever so nicely and innocently, with your eyes glowing and your face all a-shine with the wonder and expectation of it all, you inadvertently step onto the conveyor belt of an insatiable and ever-so-respectable furnace that will consume your naiveté, your clarity, and your simplicity of being, and will attempt to transform, shape, and box your spirit into something less hued and more fitting to a humorless and bottom-line society. But it's nonsense—can you see that? Green will always be the color of trees, never the color of money, and red will always be a hazy, burning, setting summer sun, never a financial deficit.

Before you send the white coats in to collar me, close your eyes again, take a deep breath, and feel what you actually are, as distinct from what you are the sum of. Let go of any tension in your body, let go of the past, the future; let go of any injury or sense of being hard done by. Let go of your job, your status, and the character you present to the world (and perhaps even to yourself) in the name of professionalism and respectability. Let go of your outrage and your seething resentment, even if just for a moment. That's who you are. That's your—the *only*—reality. Feed it, nurture it, get to know it, and it will reciprocate. Oh, you'd be surprised. It really will! For it wants to know who you are. The force that is your true reality wants to recognize you as a part of it, as *living in it*. It needs you to sink into its loving and guiding arms. It wants you to thrive.

One thing is for sure: when a question is put to you from a disembodied voice, it tends to stick. I've mused for years over these questions, as I get the feeling that they originally emanate from our own cells. They pulsate through your energy field, demanding consideration and attention.

A reasonably confrontational message came soon after, in the same fashion, just after I'd awakened. This time, I recognized the voice to be that of my female guide.

Greg, you're dying.

"But I just got married, and this is nonsense, and you're just a random voice telling me random things."

Yes, yes. I know you've just married Monika and moved to Mount Martha. In a month, you'll be dead.

"Uh, thanks for the compassion." Hmm … daren't tell Moni. She'll freak out!

Well, okay, I'd heard of ego death. You know, when you have dying dreams that apparently indicate that an aspect of you is dying. It's probably just one of those—in good old-fashioned, biblical, disembodied-voice form. Simple! So I might not be necessarily dying physically. Still, what if I am?

For the next month, I loved the world. It was less of a kick in the backside than an upending by the scruff of my neck and the seat of my pants, and a plunging of my nose into the sweet nectar of life. I was just so appreciative of every moment, color, breath of wind, scene, taste, and sound. And it was accompanied by that tremendous feeling of peace you get when you realize you're only a tourist and that all is actually very short-lived. Plus a part of me thought that I really might die.

A great way to burn of BS and a process I can highly recommend! Of course, the two messages were interrelated, and they both spoke of releasing the ego. Defining oneself through expectation and result, feeling you're a captive of the state of the world, feeling you're a captive of your own circumstances, trying to bend everything to your will—these are all aspects of the ego that only serve to hinder your true experience of being alive. As I bid the month farewell (uh, still kicking), I brushed myself off and entered the world anew, replete with tilted Panama and an array of astrally acquired Hawaiian shirts.

Had these messages been pertaining to the median wave height in the Tasman Sea, then I no doubt wouldn't have taken them to heart as much as I did or do. But, you see, these little nudging verbal gloves to the head were so personal and provocative in their simplicity that their cryptic nature only served to intensify their punch.

A few months later came the male voice again.

Greg, you lead a very unremarkable life.

"Ah, thanks heaps!" Hmm …

Chapter 13

Dominos

Greg …

"Ah … yes?"

Focus on the top of your head, where you have a slight bump.

"Ah … yes?"

Listen for a tone there. You'll hear it: a high-pitched tone.

I listened.

Now you'll hear a sequence of tones, getting progressively higher. Focus on the highest of these and when you desire to exit your body, you will separate more easily. This is an access point to the higher dimensions.

This whole prodding thing: I can't find it anything but remarkable. That we not only have inbuilt guidance software genetically installed but that it can actually interface with us in such a brazen manner. Speaking in English to my conscious, awakened mind, activating some kind of inner engine and whisking me to wherever—whenever—I intend (plus numerous bonus mystery trips to boot), showing me things, wondrous places, glorious sounds.

It all speaks to me of massive surrender. I continually see a river gliding its way through a rainforest. Boulders, trees, and the slope of the land dictate its direction and speed, the rush of the water its song. Is the river lazy for not dictating its own direction? Or is that its lot: is it in fact a victim entombed in its own form?

What is our responsibility as human beings to forge our own destiny, or is it predestined? If so, by whom or by what? These questions have occupied mankind for ages and are pivotal in shaping our experience as individuals and as a collective here on Earth. I believe the answer or the knowing lies in the child within you, that most naïve of sages.

I remember very clearly as a child perceiving my lifetime as a circle. I wanted to be whole again. I didn't even fully know what that meant, but I knew it to be so. And so my destiny was shaped—preconceived, I believe, before that first whack of the doctor's glove. *Rocks, trees, mountains ...* If you want to be clear, if you really want to be whole, you ain't got a choice, you have to go with it. Now that can either seem like a life sentence or a tremendous relief. It's up to you; it's inside you. You can force it, fight it, bend it if that's what feels right. Maybe that's your river: a canyon. But the seed is planted before you even set foot in your cot. And I know that, because whenever I've fought against it, even unwittingly, even thinking that this was my way, I've copped a lovely red ear for my efforts and have been constantly redirected—herded, even—onto the right path. I think, in the end, no matter what you're doing, you want to genuinely enjoy the experience of your life. I know it sounds inanely simplistic (and by enjoyment, I don't mean overindulgence), but I do think that's what it's all about. You just have to follow your seed, and in time, you'll remember. And it will feel good. Above all, it will feel good.

For me, all of my guidance and everything I've ever experienced tells me to let go of any plans or expectations and be constantly present. It smacks of cliché and the New Age, I know—and to those who are offended, I do apologize—but that's the truth of it. Like forever threading the eye of a needle or hugging onto a great eternal second hand of an all time-telling yet timeless clock, this window of the now is the greatest portal we have into the divine, magnificent mind of the universe. And in there, you'll see such wonders. You'll also find your greatest happiness, your ecstasy.

One morning, I woke to the words of my female guide explaining the use of a technique that would greatly aid my efforts in astral projection. It started as a dream but continued well into my waking state. As I lay there taking it all in, I hardly dared to breathe or get too excited for fear of losing transmission. She explained that at the very top of the head, there exist frequencies—a harmonic sequence of them. If we listen for and focus on the uppermost of these tones, we can effect a mind-body exit more easily.

This was learning at its best. These stories ... *I like!* And I found that she was right about the tones. At night when you lie down to sleep, or later if you're prone to wake up during the night, put your attention right to the top of your head and listen. You'll first hear some lower tones that start to get louder the more you focus on them. Then scan for higher tones, and I guarantee you, you'll start to make them out. Then go for the highest one and focus in for as long as you can. Try repeating this whole process for a few days and see what happens.

Originally, I believed these tones to be emanating from us—and perhaps they do in some form—but I'm now starting to think they could be frequencies transmitted by the universe itself. Perhaps that is the very inter-dimensional Wi-Fi signal I've been alluding to, with the receiver being in the top of our head. And to consciously focus in on the signal is akin to the fine-tuning of an old radio receiver.

Okay. Once again, I'm *given* the information. So there must be a reason for it, don't you think? It's not just random, in my opinion. And so I think that's what he was alluding to (my friendly, local disembodied male voice) when he referred to my leading an unremarkable life. Not to question further, not to explore further, and not to share further would be, to a greater degree, decidedly unremarkable. Hence my coming out. Hence this book.

Remember, this was all happening before my little Buddha had taken up residence in my belly. And things were hard. Trying to reconcile these whatever-they-weres with what was going on in my outer world was not so easy. I saw them as two distinct spheres. However, after my month's death notice, I started to feel my relationship with the outer world change. I felt the strong desire to let go of the concern for my material well-being. That doesn't mean that I didn't have to work for money. Quite the contrary. In fact, most of the work I was doing, I'd been doing for a long time, and I didn't actually want to do it. The little energy work I was doing at this time was great fun, but I wasn't able to sustain myself from it. It's hard to put a finger on it, but it was an inkling that we—as humans—were meant to be creators of our lives, not prisoners to them.

A greater part of me knew this to be true, and although it would take some time to reflect itself in my outer world, it was a certainty. It was a visceral release of something holding me within; it was the very beginning of the smile of detachment that ironically connects one to the outer world with a greater ease and grace.

When I'd get all riled up about something, it'd be done with more humor and appreciation for the drama of it. And I don't mean that in a condescending way; I just didn't feel as drained by it all. It didn't really touch me. An example of this occurred one morning when I'd arranged a meeting with the director of the department where I'd been working as a freelance music teacher. He wanted me to wear a tie, and I wanted more money. After I ran though the itemized list of how much he owed me in back pay, he responded by telling me that his hands were tied (oh, I do like that expression) as he pushed back from his desk, almost losing balance in his chair. I responded by saying, "I'll wear the noose if you pay me what I'm entitled to." We both had a chuckle and I resigned.

Do you see what I'm saying? It wasn't going to happen: the pay raise. He knew it, I knew it, but the drama was still to be enjoyed. Sure, now I had less money, and perhaps I should've gotten over my whole anti-tie stance (mmm … *nah!*), but I knew I'd acted in self-loyalty. The pay had been woefully low and the conditions were literally *smelly*. I'd acted out of fear—as in, away from fear, not in or from fear. And it wasn't just a show of pride. That job wasn't me. And there were more jobs that weren't me. And I knew that, soon, they wouldn't—*couldn't*—exist.

When I looked back over my life at the great disappointments I'd had—particularly professionally—I began to make out a pattern. At pivotal moments, when things hovered on the very precipice of success or opportunity, I'd say or do the wrong thing. Seriously, there were just too many instances. And it was as though another energy had intervened each time. Quite bizarre! Something would just come over me or the situation that would simply derail it. And looking back through newer eyes, particularly in the light of what had occurred to me since, I genuinely started to entertain the possibility of some kind of otherworldly intervention. It was at this point that I knew surrender was the only way forward—that I would find no joy if I were to continue to push at my life at all.

It came as a rush of realization that every choice I'd made and every outcome that had eventuated, every twist and turn and dead-end of my particular story, had in fact been exactly as it should have—exactly as it was or is. Without exception. And this was a tremendous release. It was ownership of my life, a total release from victimhood.

And the wall of dominos continued to tumble. Judgment—the whole good/bad thing? Perhaps things are just as they are. That doesn't mean you can't change things if you want to, but when you absorb physically the energy of judgment on an issue, are you helping yourself or the issue? I understand this may sound obtuse, but I'm getting at the idea of detachment: being nonreactive on a cellular level, not taking the judgment into your body. Does that sound cold-hearted? I put it to you that this is not the case. Quite the opposite, in fact. You'll take clearer action and see more accurately through the cloud of the situation if you're not caught up in the moral outrage of it all. It actually gives you more space to act from the heart.

That's what I'm referring to when I speak of the irony of detachment: your inner and outer worlds will actually mesh more seamlessly when you release your dependence on the result (the representation of the situation in the outer world) and focus instead on the perfection that exists within you. Whoops! Let the cat out of the bag then, didn't I? You see, we're all perfect beings.

You can't *not* come to that realization when you've spent as much time in the astral as I have. The universe is benevolent, is *loving*—simple as that. And remember, the inner world precedes the outer world, not vice versa, just as an idea or notion precedes an action. Why would it be any different with the world? Energy always precedes matter and will continue to exist long after. Go within, find the peace, recognize your perfection by totally accepting yourself, act from the heart, and project that into the illusion: the outer world.

The human world can do with some release right now. It's our responsibility—and birthright—to let the genie out of the bottle. In my case, it's a fat little Buddha who snores, eats, and laughs very loudly.

CHAPTER 14

Duty or Love?

The clouds are above.
I'm through them.
Face hard against the speed;
I've stopped.
The planet below pulsates and strains,
It's holding it together.
Just …

I once found myself looking back at the Earth from around the distance of the moon. I was seeing the energy of the Earth. Now this was a few years back, before we strapped on the global-warming handle. Our planet was pulsating, struggling to breathe. I could see bands of light circumnavigating the globe that seemed to be flexing, straining, and reverberating in particularly reddish colors. I could feel physically (or more correctly, astrally, a stronger feeling than the physical) the desperation of the Earth. It was suffering, and it was calling out.

This was early on in my astral career, and to be honest, I hadn't given that much genuine thought to this particular theme before (apart from a few clever and colorful school projects), and so I was quite shocked, upset, and moved by this experience. Can you see the power in such learning? Remember, I'm looking back at the globe in ultra-high-definition, seeing these bands superimposed around the Earth, and watching them vibrate and shudder while knowing, feeling, sensing the struggle and frustration of the planet. This is experiential education at its best, even though it's not about learning per se, it's about experiencing or being one with. In the space of a few minutes, my whole attitude toward our planet underwent a metamorphosis. I realized that it was our *home*, our mother. It existed as an entity, and that entity was in trouble.

So now, when I remove a plastic bag from the sea, I'm not doing it to be good or correct in some way; the action requires no effort or ideology. I simply do it. It's beyond choice, judgment, or mere decision-making; it's the natural flow of connectedness. The Earth, you, and I are all part of the same story. Wouldn't you remove a plastic bag from your head if it was suffocating you?

I believe this to be the crux of our flailing relationship with the Earth: pronouncements like "Political correctness dictates that we should or must do this or that to solve the spiraling problem of global warming." Very important sounding stuff indeed! (Rule no. 1: if it sounds overly important, can it! Rule no. 2: if it sounds too emotive—"should," "must"—also can it!) All this rhetoric only serves to widen the gap further between ourselves and the Earth. It separates us; it says we're not *of* it, as well as clouding the real issue.

We shouldn't, mustn't anything! If it really requires any kind of effort to do something, then you really have to take a good look at the motives you're serving and question them. Do you think your organs are wind-bagging amongst themselves about how much of an effort it is to keep you alive?

Imagine if divinity classes at school focused on developing a sense of connectedness with our world instead of coloring in Joseph on his donkey. Perhaps Christianity has been misunderstood or deliberately misinterpreted? For example, who among you have sacrificed or are sacrificing your passion in life to support the notion of being a good person? Love or duty? As everything is in the interpretation, does the word *sacrifice* make your body feel good or feel cramped? Close your eyes and test it out, for your cells won't lie. They're in this together with you; they *are* you. And they are blind to the notions of sacrifice or effort.

Many of my friends jump up and down when I talk about the individual being the center of their universe. Out of breath and with faces all a-crease, they tell me that we have to forget about ourselves (for once!) and get to the task of saving the Earth. True and noble warriors, they're aghast at the indifference of humanity to the Earth's plight. And they do have a point. But I question their motive: it reeks of separation and often serves to feed the militant appetite within them and their organizations. To a degree, it may work for them, but any service must truly come from a place of love. Otherwise, it'll eat you up from the inside out, define and alienate you. The true essence of our relationship with the environment is exactly that: a *relationship*. As the major impactors of the Earth in this epoch, we'd do better by rediscovering that this connection lies within us, nurturing it, and acting from a sense of oneness and wonder rather than correctness (such a clipped and merciless word, devoid of any humanity—yet one defining our age).

✳   ✳   ✳

And so my journeys out of the body continued, as did my wonder and awe at the great creative energy or spirit that contains—*is*—us. A discussion on spirituality with a French monk (who actually spoke English with an accent) was followed the next night by a private audience with a man who chanted. But boy, what chanting! I watched and marveled as he intoned words and sounds I'd never heard before. The intensity—his voice's absolute connection with the source—was hypnotic and all-consuming. I thought, how am I watching this man? Can he see me or can I only see him? At song's end, he lifted his head, opened his eyes, and turned slightly to meet my gaze. In the next few seconds, as our eyes locked, I discovered much about who and what I was or could be, and I felt that a pact had been made between myself and the source. The ball was now in my court, and the golden key of true creativity dangled before me in all its mystery and magic.

I began to realize that the perfect state was always within; it was never absent. It was home, and it was always there. When the wind blew and the hail roared all around us, this inner bliss remained, immovable yet in constant awe. This was the true reality; this was the natural state of being. And it required no effort, no straining.

It was around this time that my laughing Buddha took up residence in my belly. Or rather, he de-cloaked himself so that I could actually recognize him to be there. This was no mere concept or play of my imagination; he was actually there. So clear and so real. There he was with his bulging head and his bulging cheeks and his bulging tummy having an absolute time of it. So odd, yet so strangely comforting. Even as I write this and would have liked to describe the minimalist clothing around his groin in a perhaps slightly less coy fashion, I see him ever so subtly straightening himself up as if to caution me against the improper use of a certain expression—albeit lovingly. You see, I sincerely wish him no disrespect. But he *is* there, and he *is* real; as real, in fact, as the very breath that at this moment sustains you. Yet both are what we would call invisible.

And so to the illusion: that most glorious of stages, where giant feathered hats are ceremoniously tipped with a flourish and quizzical pouts are met with unending applause; where your life can be in the cut of a shoe or the hem of a jacket; where intellect is oft confused with intelligence and importance with quality; where food is unashamedly poisoned in the name of righteous profit; where ignorance is kind of hip and savvy; where the hungry play scapegoat to our mysterious sense of guilt and political posturing (rather than actually being fed); where the reflection on a leaf can lift you spellbound with joy, and the flight of an errant plastic bag can tickle your fancy yet fill you with panic all at the same time. What a majesty of reflection it is! What a poem of wonder and what potential for creativity. Can you see it's all a dance of our soul—a getting to know ourselves? Do we want to see something else? It's all our creation, so let's own it, just as we should own our leaders and their policies, rather than cussing and blaming them. After all, we brought them into creation, didn't we? And so it is with our world. What do we want to see?

It is my belief that we are created in the image of the Great Creative Energy, which many of us call God. How could we not be? We carry the very same pulsation of that initial ecstatic creative release that science terms the Big Bang (a banal and wonder-less expression, to my mind, that denigrates the first great burst of creative energy to the realms of celestial pornography) within us. Now as you've no doubt gathered, I'm not a great fan of religion. Bloodshed and dogma are not my thing, but one cannot fail to recognize the essence of the same Great Creative Energy threaded throughout them all. My argument with Christianity, the religion I was raised in, is that I am God—we are God. It's not outside of us, nor does it have to be reached through an intermediary. The trees are God, as are the fish and every living being, including rocks. You think rocks are not alive and buzzing with energy? Put them under a microscope. Things are moving in there! Scientists spend billions of dollars looking for life on other planets. Are they mad? I put it to you that every thing, every thought, every possibility, every action is alive. They're all God. How could they not be infused with creation's great ecstatic surge?

Now the reason I'm sharing this with you is that these were the feelings flooding though me in the lead-up to a truly unusual and gravity-defying astral/normal-waking-state experience. I started to recognize the universe for the playground that it was, as opposed to the schoolroom that had been fed into the illusion. The chalkboard was gone, the teacher's pointing stick had dropped to the floor, shattering into a million brittle shards, and the four stifling inhibiting walls had collapsed in their own Big Bang of dust and release. Our role was to *be* the creator, to discover our true powers of being, and to play with them—to create our own reality.

CHAPTER 15

The Roaring

Levitate (verb): rise or cause to rise and hover
in the air, especially by means of supernatural
or magical power.—*Oxford Dictionaries*

The day started out like any other. After being greeted by a clear, sunny morning, I should have felt more excited, as I'd planned to go camping for a couple of days at a well-known surf beach a couple of hours' drive away from Melbourne. But I didn't feel that good. In fact, a really dark sense of gloom had me in its hold, and I questioned whether I should go through with the trip after all. Something was coming my way, that was for sure, and it was going to change everything.

After some discussion on the topic with my wife, we eventually decided to leave. I drove very carefully—to avoid the obvious—but on arrival at the campsite, the feeling of dread and uneasiness only intensified. Do you see, the experience was already in my energy field.

I could have acted upon it earlier by pulling out of the trip altogether, but my curiosity had fueled me to play it out to the end. Did you know that if you take a cutting from a plant, its energy field flares into survival mode (panic mode) before you even touch the plant? It knows beforehand. And so it is with us: before any experience, including illness or injury, solidifies in the material body, its presence is felt in the energetic bodies—the astral vehicle being one of these bodies and one of the closest in density to the physical.

My sense of foreboding had reached crescendo point by the time I paddled out to meet the breaking waves. Yet I must confess that a part of me was fascinated by what was going on. The sense of detachment that had been building within me over time enabled me to enjoy—in a strange kind of way—the process of whatever was happening as it unfolded, albeit from an otherworldly vantage point. It was the existential paradox encapsulated. It was paddling out on a beautiful sunny day, under a staring black sky.

As I took the drop and watched the wave unfold, I could sense the strings tightening around my form. Where was I being taken and by whom? What was I going to see now? As though from above, I watched impassively as my board hit the bump halfway down the wave and my left (front) leg lost its footing. As the board rose up to meet my body, I felt the twang of a string in my left knee as the foot slipped and skipped forward across the wet and waxy deck. I was off my board now, and time and space were fast again. And loud. I had to get back to my board, but my leg was dangling funny in the water. Paddle in, catch some white water, and then I was done.

The doctor was able to get the knee back into the joint, but it was crutches for six weeks and then a probable operation after further assessment. I liked the doctor's approach: when I asked him for a candid prognosis, he smiled a big question mark back at me and said "Who knows …?" I appreciated the lack of a label. Somewhere in the back of my mind, a door had been left open. We decided to camp the night anyway. The leg was strapped, the tent was up, the weather was good, and the pain was bearable. Why leave?

The tent actually felt cozy with the cool night air blowing in from the ocean. But it was difficult to get into a comfortable position under the sleeping bag. I found that if I lay on my back (the best position for astral traveling, by the way) and kept the knee slightly elevated, the pain wasn't too pronounced, and I might be able to get some sleep. I relaxed my body as much as I could, brought in Reiki, and asked for all the help I could get. Perhaps my guides could lend a helping hand?

As I lay there, listening to the wind and the sounds of the surf on the shore, I thought about the illusion. Was this not it? Wasn't my knee coexisting within me in a perfect state somewhere? Wasn't there a template somewhere in my energy field that I could draw from to heal my leg? All I had to do was to access it, to believe it and to know it into being.

I knew that if I could carry this knowledge into my sleep state, without losing consciousness, I had a chance at something happening. If I could just cross the threshold of sleep, where the logical mind unravels, and enter the astral carrying even a portion of this knowing, what powers could be unleashed?

And so I began my mantra, the best way to cross an intention into the invisible realms, the true reality: *I deny the illusion of my injured knee and give thanks for my perfect health. I deny the illusion of my injured knee and give thanks for my perfect health. I deny the illusion of my injured knee and give thanks for my perfect health.*

For the next two hours, I lay there, on my back, repeating these words over and over, taking them into my being, letting them resonate through me. Whenever I'd feel my consciousness slipping off into a random sleep state and the words muddling themselves, I'd pull myself back and resume the chant. Over and over and over. And while doing this, I sensed my energy body within and around me, in all its perfection, reminding my physical body—reminding my knee—of its normal, perfect state. It felt good to do this. And it felt relaxing. It wasn't difficult or requiring of any particular effort. It felt right.

At some stage, I must have entered sleep. I don't remember crossing the threshold, but I wasn't deterred, as this often happened when projecting astrally. It was like powering up a lawn mower, where you keep pulling the chord: the effect is cumulative. It's the planting of the intention—or the knowing—into your inner hard drive.

I slept surprisingly deeply for most of the night, waking only a few times and each time continuing on with the mantra, as the focus also helped me to release the pain in the knee and diffuse the panic at the discomfort of not being able to move from my position on my back. Just after dawn, I'd had enough, and I began to mount a campaign to roll onto my stomach. Ever so gently, I attempted to peel my body caterpillar style, one section at a time, onto its front. After the usual transit pangs, the leg began to feel better as I sought out a position where the kneecap felt quasi-supported by the mattress. (Thank God we brought the foam mattresses!)

And that was when it started: the roaring.

At first I felt the usual astral engine whirring into action, this feeling I'd felt many times before as an internal body waking from its slumber and sending a welcome charge of vibrations though my being. But this was different: I was still physically awake. I opened my eyes wide and the vibrations continued. Then came the roar. If you've ever heard a bullroarer, it was like that, max to the ten. It was an all-encompassing, deep-throated, centrifugal roar. And I was in the middle of it, eyes open, aghast.

My wife is lying next to me, all is as it should be with the tent, and my heart is pounding furiously. As the roar increases its frequency, I feel the weight of my body against the mattress inexplicably lighten and then I am quite nimbly yet uniformly lifted by some invisible force and rotated onto my back before being gently placed back down onto the mattress.

Then come the words—*in my voice*. I am lying on my back listening to my own voice speak through what seems to be some kind of resonator as it matches the intensity of the roar. And the words, well, they are to shock me: *Our Father, who art in heaven, hallowed be thy name. Thy kingdom come, thy will be done on Earth as it is in heaven ...*

As the voice reaches these last two lines, the roar intensifies even more, and they seem to repeat over and over (these last two lines) with the roar accompanying them, as though in chorus. And during this process, I feel what seems to be many fingertips in and around my knee—prodding, pressing, manipulating—at what appears to be lightning speed. And while the rest of the prayer is also being incanted, the two lines "Thy will be done on Earth, as it is in heaven" seem to reverberate simultaneously above the rest.

Keep calm, keep calm. It's okay, it's good. Close your eyes and relax.

Well, I can't close my eyes. I lie there stiff with fright, yet at the same time infused with this wonderful energy pulsating all through and around my body. I fix my gaze on the roof of my tent, not daring to glance in the direction of all the activity around my knee.

The Lord's Prayer? Sure, I knew it as a kid, but if you asked me to recite it, I'm not sure I could.

And then come the hands around the feet and ankles, applying gentle pressure—before the big pull.

"Nah, I'm outa here." Abort. Shake my legs and wake my wife. Call me a wimp, but I am wide awake, and this is really freaky. Good but too much. I'm not ready for that!

In retrospect, I'd have to say it was a pity I couldn't have just toughed it out a bit longer. Who knows what might have happened had I just surrendered? However, the upshot of it was that I dumped the crutches after ten days and never had to have the operation. The leg healed very well and very quickly, and I was back to playing squash within six months.

And I know that something happened that wondrous morning in that tent by the sea; something mystical, yet way beyond the grasp of any kind of logic. Perhaps it was time to let the logical go? There was a whole other world to tap into here, just below the surface. The fact that my body had levitated and turned over in full waking consciousness; the searching and prodding fingertips; and the hands around my ankles ... what were they about to show me, and where were they about to take me? In a way that was clear to me—and in another way that wasn't—I had managed to summon up invisible forces that had defied the physical constraints of conventional scientific thinking. Intellect had fallen down the rabbit hole. The Earth and this 3-D reality had altered their definitions in a place deep within me that never forgets. For a moment—for just a sparkling, dangling, incomprehensibly beautiful moment—the astral world had unmasked itself to show me its true face, that of the primary reality.

And what of the Lord's Prayer? Well, there must be something in it. I believe an incantation voiced and sounded out into the ether over hundreds of years will take on a power all of its own. And I do think that is the power of religion, particularly in those societies where people really *feel* it and live it as opposed to the cardboard cutout version that many seem to adhere to for respectability's sake. The fact that I had recited it in a voice that was ostensibly mine but that had emanated from another dimension of greater knowing and with the seeming ability to call up unseen forces to interact with, and manipulate, the 3-D dimension of form, was for me further proof as to the existence of a higher or sovereign self that coexists consciously and actively alongside and within our mortal framework. *Thy will be done on Earth, as it is in heaven …*

By far the majority of the mass of the human body is oxygen, as it is with our atmosphere. When you look outside of yourself, you mainly see space, as in *room*. So it is with our bodies: we're mainly room. My perception of myself as a solid being has altered so dramatically over the past decade or so, it allows me—no, *invites* me—to sense myself more as a flow and expanse of porous energy, interacting with all around me, visible and invisible. And once again, it's not a theory I've learned or studied or want to believe in or belong to. I feel it—I *am* it. The tent experience only served to harden my resolve to delve further into the mystery of what it truly means to be human.

Chapter 16

Creating Reality

> Mantra (noun): a word or sound repeated to
> aid concentration in meditation. *Origin* late
> 18th century: Sanskrit, literally "a thought,
> thought behind speech or action," from
> *man-* "think."—*Oxford Dictionaries*

The whole concept of the repeated mantra or prayer is an interesting thing—that words and lines can become so infused with intensity and mystical energy. You can imagine monks in whatever religion, mind and body in total absorption using the spoken word to propel a request, an intention, a state of being out into the great, immutable, invisible (for the most part) expanse/body of the universe. You can imagine seeing the words, the earnest intentions, the actual vibrations flying forth from the Earth's surface and meshing with the great universal current of consciousness. And these same words, over hundreds of years ...

And so it is with our own thoughts and words. What is the story mankind has been sending out—feeding—into our universe? How many times, for example, have you repeated the mantra *I can't afford it* from the very core of your being? Do you realize you're actually enlivening energy into substance, into form, by constantly affirming this state of being? Western society's obsession with focusing on the negative—the killings, the victims, the disasters, the tragedies, the *loss*—only expands and breathes greater life (or death) into this mistaken way of thinking and being. As a result, we hunger for it in our entertainment and our daily life. We unconsciously thirst for constriction, as we believe this lack to *be* us. How many of you have a genuine attraction for genuinely appalling food, for example? Do you really believe your cells will not absorb the lack or the poisons that are contained within it? Do you not feel it? Or do you simply not care? Do you actually read or research the list of ingredients? If so, then why the death wish?

The ego, which is fear alone and seemingly ingrained into the human energy field, *is* this apathy, *is* the lack. The ego, which thrives on separation and the glee of misfortune (particularly others', but also our own), is an interloper and the prime culprit behind humanity's mass hypnosis and the endless cycle of human reincarnation into form. Once we wake up to the true nature of reality, it's a dead duck. Feel it within you, stare it down, and don't react to it. It may panic a little, but just continue to starve it and keep oxygen from it. Stay non-reactive, even hesitate a little if you have to, and begin to respond from how you might actually feel as opposed to how your default character normally responds. Keep doing this, and your ego will literally deflate; it'll start to cower. Give it time, and be patient with yourself. And one day, *ping*—you've snapped the chord and you will recognize it (the ego) to be entirely separate from you and not *of* you. And you will be entirely present.

When this happens, your thinking will release itself, and you may just surprise yourself as you begin to take breath from an expanded and vitalized field of consciousness. For example, you may begin to feel compassion for not only the victims of crime but for the so-called criminals as well, as the formerly reactive and blinkered, black-and-white, this-or-that approach flies out the window of limited and purely constructed emotive thinking. At this point, your heart begins to gain confidence at the rudder, and its view is deeper and more telling as the seething cloud of outrage and oppression within you begins to dissipate and clear. And there will be no turning back. You will recognize the concept of hell to be manmade and see its reflection in our own punishment system, where the apparent sinner within us must be made to suffer, instead of being healed in some way or even loved. You will begin to sense that the "eye for an eye and a tooth for a tooth" induced madness of so-called karma is actually our own doing, our own creation, and the very engine of unconscious reactivity that powers our unceasing return into the realm of form and 3-D consciousness, as in our current physical reality. With your new way of thinking, you'll have discovered the key to standing outside of the current of the reactive human experience, while at the same time bathing in its ecstatic ebb and flow.

*   *   *

What has struck me most about many of the beings I've met in the astral dimensions is their intensity. I don't mean fervor or the madness of frothing conviction—I mean an intensity in their presence. They're really *there*. And you often see this characteristic in people of our reality who have somehow mastered their own energies enough to create the life they want. Often, very fulfilled people carry this trait of near absolute presence. Perhaps a relationship exists between the focus of intent they emanate into the ether and the clarity in which life seems to be reflected back to them. Now there's nothing particularly new or groundbreaking in what I'm saying here; what I am attempting to point out is that most of us appear to be energetically fractured. We seem particularly distracted in the way we engage in life. We thirst for a 3-D reality and think we'll only find it in cinemas. We see everything as being outside of ourselves, and we think we need more to be more.

Sure, a consumer society may thrive from this continuum, and we all love our stuff, but just what are we missing out on in return? Is it enough to merely skate along the surface of being and have a two-dimensional reality (that so many seem unhappy with) beamed back at us? Cause and effect: *this* is the true definition of karma, not the blame-game definition that the West has fallen so heavily for. Why the need to feel guilty anyway? I know I'm asking a lot of questions, but I'm so puzzled at the supposed outrage expressed by people—which is generally of the politically correct, manufactured, robotic variety—at the state of the world, when behind their eyes, all I can see is the panic of perhaps missing a scene from their favorite TV show. The notion that we're creating it all as we go along—that the words, the intentions, the appetites that inhabit our being are being fed back to us—is the furthest thing from their minds. To rectify the situation is seemingly irrelevant; it's the outrage that counts. As a species, we're on automatic pilot. We've fallen in love with this sense of outrage, we've embraced victimhood as our trusted friend, and we've hypnotized ourselves into seeing a human lifetime as a prison sentence. Why?

You know it's not all relative out there. A life defined by a purely external, whiz-bang, "look at me" ethos is never going to give you that sense of completeness and well-being that we all do crave. I put it to you that the default setting of the universe is a state of ecstatic bliss; and no, I've never been to an Indian ashram, nor do I sit around all day cross-legged (even though I think both could be a good idea). I say this because I've *felt* it, I've *been* it when I've entered the astral dimensions. And as we literally *are* the universe in human form, it is also our default setting—and it will out. It's what we are, and it's so easy to see. For example, just look at a person who has ruled his life purely by monetary profit (I won't say wealth, as that is another thing all together) at the expense of human decency. Money that is made knowingly on the back of human suffering or death, money that is made knowingly at the expense of our health, money that is made knowingly to the detriment of the environment—just look at the physical manifestation of such people who have profited in such a corruptive way, and you will see a corrupted organism. They will look unwell. The inner is reflected in the outer, as with everything. Surely you've all noticed this. I'm often bewildered by the fact that, although we live in a particularly visual society, people seemingly fail to observe this most obvious and blatant law of universal nature. Do you really look? Can you really see? Let me elect a leader based purely on the physical manifestation of his or her being, and I guarantee you it'll be a better choice than one based on the mere expertness of her rhetoric and the cleverness of his sneer. So as I said earlier, it's not relative, nor is it open for interpretation. We want to be well, and those who do not serve this inner universal yearning are unwell. So be it.

*   *   *

And so it made sense to hear the Lord's Prayer rather than some pithy fast-food mantra, even though both would be penetrating the great universal consciousness, which is us. I guess my cells felt more resonance with the former's intention, even though I don't wave the Christian flag aloft. If the intention is pure, the casing of a particular religion around it is irrelevant, as our cells know no bias. They're not clever enough, nor are they well-read enough—they simply recognize an affirmation of life-force energy when they hear it. A vibration, whether it be a thought, an intention, or a word (as all of these precede an action), is either for us or against us. And the *for* will win out each time. No relativity, no compromise, simply the universe in creation—for it only knows, *is*, benevolence.

Would you vote for a president or prime minister who would not allow your country to engage in military invasions of other sovereign states? I would. And dearly so. Any chance at a world without war is a good one. "Oh, but the Chinese will invade and kill us all!" Well then, I'm prepared to take that gamble. You may think the worst-case scenario would be to be killed, but what if I tell you we are already living in a worst-case scenario, in an illusory continuum of fear and killing? As you read this now, somewhere in the world, in the name of ideology and under the righteous flag of an invading state, someone—a father, a mother, a brother, a sister, a child—is being murdered with a feigned sneer of contempt (*feigned* as in fraught with fear). It might not be right in front of you, perhaps not even on your 3-D TV, but it's happening all the same. And even though you can't see it, it's not making you feel good. I guarantee that: it's not making any of us feel good. I would choose not to live in such a realm, if push came to shove, and move on with my immortal spirit to one that lives in a greater truth than ours. For me, the risk entails life, not death. What would you choose? If you choose war from the sterility and comfort of your leather couch, replete with myriad remote controls, then you choose also to be, to carry the energy of, the perpetrator and the killer. And if so, own it, embrace it, and accept that this is the reality you've chosen. But in so doing, you will never feel truly free, nor well, for this ethos germinates from an illusory soil infested with fear, suffering, and the energy of lack, and permeates our collective consciousness as a dark and inhibiting weed. This is true devil worship.

I was once standing by my bed with the moonlight streaming through the window, just looking down at my sleeping self. It can be quite frightening to do, as you almost don't recognize yourself or for some reason don't want to. But I wanted to explore this sensation, this feeling, for a little while longer, as I felt there was something here I had to come to terms with. As I pored over my facial features and physical form in a state of half-shock and quasi-disgust, I felt something alter within me as a feeling of empathy for my poor defenseless and solid shell came over me. Empathy for myself—a strange phenomenon indeed. You see, with each line on my face, with every feature and every fleshy and strange undulation, there was a story that was so clearly seen in the light of the astral eye. I felt compassion for the false sense of vulnerability etched so severely in the brow and cheek lines, and for the illusory belief in failure and restriction in the tilt of the chest and the curve of the shoulders. The body wore the mistaken garland of separation and limited thinking, and my heart went out to it.

Ironically, it is our very bodies—which represent the world of the material to us in its most personal manifestation—that play the greater and overriding role as the conduit to the inner realms of true power. Yet as we continue to ignore this true nature, the obsession with the protection of the physical "it" and of all bodies (of government and of folk, for example) has spun itself into a kind of insane hyperdrive, seemingly to excuse the most irrational of thinking and of acts against ourselves and at the same time supporting and feeding further the myth of our separation and mortality. Why do we despise ourselves so? Are we in fact punishing ourselves for our alleged fall into form? Are we all sinners at heart?

Our repeated offerings or mantras of apocalyptic self-destruction and self-sacrifice that Hollywood seems to spin out untiringly into the galactic ether (that either the Earth hates us and is going to kill us, or outer space hates us and is going to kill us) remind me of the self-absorbed and frustrated little boy who, with the game not going his way, beats up and destroys what he can of the scene before returning home with the bat and the ball so that nobody else can play without him. Sure, it's been said before and it'll be said many times again, but a little self-love can go so far and give such repair to our bruised and flagellated collective body. And a lot of self-love ... well, that will be our making, won't it?

One day we'll all go home—we seem to all know that instinctively, without really quite believing it—but rather than giving up on us just yet, why not bring to the game here on Earth a lushness that has nothing to do with an economic-bottom-line mentality? Why not close your eyes and think how nice it feels to be alive, even when yet another reported death from the war is thrust into your energy field? How about, instead of thinking "Aren't they terrible?" as you react to 99 percent of reported daily "news" stories, you think "Aren't they beautiful?" That's really going to mess with your ego, isn't it? That's basically akin to spinning it around your head a few times at high velocity and releasing it headfirst into the nearest brick wall, a practice most recommendable and entirely effective. I think Jesus even mentioned it when he referred to loving your enemy. I think he was onto something. And it's not about taking or blindly accepting crap, it's about recognizing the truth or true spirit in everyone and reacting to that rather than the default jostling of the ego into its beloved, yet immensely ho-hum, outrage stance. It's about having empathy for the human condition and the frailties that come with it. Such basic, uncomplicated, and seemingly unimportant words, yet they birth feelings within that resonate with the very mind of the universe. They are the mantras that form the unimaginable into the imaginable. And they are our tools to create a paradise free from lack, bloodlust, sacrifice, punishment, and duty—if we want it. That's what we're all about; that's why we're here. It's our choice. It's your choice.

A mundane yet nevertheless powerful mantra we all use without even noticing it to be one is "hooray, hooray, hooray." Not only is this very similar in sound to the Reiki power symbol, but it is also stated emphatically three times and bears a dramatic aural resemblance to an ancient Mongolian shamanic praise mantra (also stated thrice). And if you think about what this ritual entails in our society, the well-wishing of another year lived and the blessing of many more to come, or the praise of a winning accomplishment, in a form that is not quietly spoken, person to person, but sung in loving chorus, announced to the universe in unequivocal joy—who cannot fail to feel good about such a ritual? Such rituals and mantras exist all around us in our modern societies, having filtered down from ancient wisdom and knowing. They may have become unconscious in their use, but they are still powerful tools and expressions of being, as they connect instinctively with the very fabric of the universe.

And so I have learned to adapt these techniques to gain access to other realities. First, I will voice the intention of consciously leaving my body: "Tonight, I am going to consciously leave my body." I'll say this three times. Each time I say it, my body reacts differently, as though it's sitting up and taking notice. By the third time, it's saying, *Okay, okay, I getcha*, and nodding its head in that hip, *comprende* kind of fashion. Now remember, I see the mind and body as one; I don't differentiate between the two. You need to take your intentions inside of you, where they really twang. Feel them bouncing all around your innards. Your organs do a lot more than merely keep your body turning over. They're all part of your mind. They have things to tell you—in fact, they're constantly speaking to you—and they all play a vital role in your power centers (your chakras), which in turn help to power and project the energetic double, your astral journeyer. Turn inward a lot and get to feel the flow of energy through you.

Now what is it you want to see or experience? What do you want to know? Feel the desire for this experience engulf your whole being and repeat the request inwardly a few times to yourself. Ask for help!

Oh, there are energies out there that will help you, you know—you just need to engage them.

As you lie there on your back with your eyes closed, you'll begin to feel more and more relaxed in your body. Imagine you're a cork submerged in water. Feel yourself being pulled to the surface. It's time to start seeing yourself as the energy inhabiting your body as distinct from pure physicality. See yourself hovering around six feet above your body. Now put your consciousness in the hovering body. Rotate and watch yourself lying in bed from above. Look closely at your face. If need be, flit your consciousness down to just above your forehead and look down your body from this position. How does your face look from just outside your left ear? Your right ear? How does your body look from just above your head? Now go back up to the hovering body and look back down at yourself. Your face, the sheets, the bed, the room … how does it all look?

Do you see what you're doing here? You're reminding your consciousness that it can exist away from the physical body. Our materialistic age has thrived on the precept that we are purely material beings, and we've truly forgotten what we are: immortal spirit and undying consciousness. It'll feel scary at first—somehow wrong, being away from the body. But that's just cellular and past-life memory kicking in. For hundreds of years, humans were burned at the stake and tortured in the most gruesome ways for exhibiting knowledge of their true spirit. This is not fable. Look into it. It really happened, and we remember it on a certain level. You will not suddenly die or be possessed by another entity when you leave your body, nor is it devil worship. Open a door of possibility somewhere in your mind; allow just the idea of it to be possible. That is the first step to what I suppose is (dare I say it) a vehicle to personal enlightenment.

You're planting the seed now, and the unconscious mind will begin to unravel it while you sleep. Before you fall asleep, though, remain conscious of your consciousness. That may sound obtuse, but what I mean is, sense your being and when you feel your mind starting to slide into a story or when you sense it fracturing into other characters, reel it back in and remind yourself of your presence—and sense your being. Do this repeatedly and you'll start to get flashes of light as the veil of illusion begins to part. At some stage, when you've had enough, let yourself fall asleep.

Another technique I like to use is to simply focus your sight onto the inside of your eyelids. What you'll see is what I take to be some kind of static electricity that shows itself as dull swirls or strains of light. Focusing on these moving patterns for some time will distract you from falling asleep, and eventually, if you keep pulling yourself back from the brink of losing consciousness, you may find the light concentrating and brightening into the center of your view until round, intense flashes can occur. Stay with this, if you can, because it can precipitate astral exits if your body has already fallen asleep.

Now what will happen if you really keep at this for some time is that at some stage, an aspect of your consciousness is going to cotton on to your desire and wake you when it deems appropriate. It will wake you *while you continue to sleep*. A paradox and a half, eh? And this will be your astral body, at your service.

When this happens, you have two options. Either think nothing and let the body take you somewhere and show you something, or ask for what it is you want to see or experience. Sometimes you'll be prompted to ask for something—this is when the astral body goads you into remembering what it was you were wanting to do, before you got astral stage fright and started energetically blubbering the equivalent of "Say what?"

Then see what happens. The first time it does happen to you, you'll be changed forever and for good.

CHAPTER 17

Feeling It

I'm soaring up the valley almost too quickly to take
anything in. Stay low, stay low. The trees, the rocky
formations, the valley's fingers opening out to the right and
left—I take them all in, seemingly in an instant. I know the
trenches, the gullies, the streams, the snowdrifts. I'm intimate
with each leaf and texture. A million fingertips caressing the
speeding scene below me and vice versa. It's all so fast, yet
there is an inexpressible stillness about it.

You'll never be in danger of not returning to your body during
or after an astral experience. I remember when I first started
experimenting in all of this, a healer friend berated me, saying it was
much too dangerous to try this alone and without proper guidance.
I would read on websites that evil entities could enter your body at
the point of separation and lock you out of your own body, dooming
you to an eternity of corporeal homelessness in the murky domains

of the lower astral. I love these sorts of theories. *I love to prove them wrong.* It's simply not going to happen. You will always be safe. I actually guarantee it.

I believe what has happened in these instances is that illusory monsters in the lower astral realms have scared the bejeebers out of those unconsciously venturing into them, especially as they cross the threshold of realities. They are just manifestations of fear projected into this realm to test your resolve. Find your way around them; you won't regret it.

Possession by another entity is something else entirely and has a lot to do with a fractured and extremely disturbed personality. It has nothing to do with gaining conscious control of a mechanism that is both natural and healing—namely astral projection.

It appears that for some reason, a lot of people are vested in this hidden and forgotten sense of ours remaining just that: hidden and forgotten. Imagine the unleashed potential of the human race when we reignite this inner sense. Who has the most to lose by releasing the astral genie out of the bottle? I'm convinced that we are here to experience the divine right of creation that sparks within us. Astral travel, or projection, is merely a side effect of your consciousness punching its way through the illusory wall of what we perceive to be the true and only reality. Once the bricks and mortar begin to fall away, the energy behind *this* so-called reality pushes to the fore to reveal itself in all its unadorned glory. For example, a product designed for profit will only (can only) pass onto you, the consumer, the energy of that desired profit. You will feel it, sense it, see it, because that's what it is, what it's designed for: profit. It's not necessarily designed for *you*; it gives you nothing. In fact, if the intention is purely for profit, it will take away from you in some way; it will damage you. Many of the major food-industry concerns operate from this space of no heart and, in so doing, along with your unconscious complicity (it would seem), succeed in deliberately poisoning the human race while feverishly lining their pockets.

That's not to say that all profit is bad. Far from it! If the primary intention is to help the human race in some way—to better an existing condition in some form or another—then the energy carried through the product or service will actually give you something, as in, have a positive effect on you. Can you see the simplicity in that? For me, it's no theory, it's energy: palpable, visible, visceral, and utterly reliable. I call it *reality*.

And it is the using of these tools that will prime your astral body into conscious action and vice versa. It's a self-perpetuating, self-sharpening system. The next time you buy a product, note how you feel: *elated, relaxed, content, disgusted, nauseated*. How does it make you feel? And why, do you think? I remember years ago, eating a burger from a certain famous fast-food outlet. Actually, it was McDonald's, and I wondered why I felt so sickly afterward even though I'd craved it so. This pattern went on for some time, until it dawned upon me that the food wasn't good for me. So I stopped eating it. So simple and so effective, yet seemingly so unreliable a tool for so many of us: our feelings. Begin to honor them, little by little, even if it means being a little bit different or swimming against the current, and a new world will open up to you. I guarantee it. For you see, these feelings will get stronger and stronger within you, entering the realms of utter reliability as you step into your truth—the only truth, in fact.

How does it make us feel? This is the biggest question the human race can ask itself right now. No, it's not the most important one (as suggested earlier, if it sounds overly important, can it!), yet it remains hovering above us in the true reality of the Earth's ether, like a giant heavenly ear, patiently cupped in the silence of the eons—listening, listening, listening for an answer.

And as a collective, we must start with ourselves, as individuals. That person, that situation, that job, that food, that house, that new law … how does it make you feel?

Now here's the catch. Every time you choose not to honor your true feelings and remain inert to them, you sink deeper into the realm of the collective unconscious. You feed the dragon and in so doing you only serve to add to the bloat and gloat of the greatest masquerade and hoax of all time: fear. And it's this perceived fear (perceived, as it doesn't actually exist) that will keep you down, that will stop you from developing your senses, that will by compliance allow the pure profiteers of the world to continue dumbing us down and poisoning our systems and our Earth. It's a continuum, one that we must wake up to. And it's so, so simple to do. Simply act on your feelings.

Each time you act from a place of your truth, from your feelings, you eliminate fear and dead thinking from your consciousness and, by extension, the collective consciousness of the human race. You honor yourself and, in so doing, give true meaning to what it means to be human, for we are not instinctively evil, you know. You do know? It is an emergence from the great sea of paralysis—the self-discovery of your own two feet. And you'll find that the ornately adorned, convoluted, and ever-so-highly respected columns of reality based on perpetuated fear and oppression will crumble into the lightest, most unspectacular dust without so much as a thud. And then you'll feel it, really feel it: the smile within you.

You see, you're lightening the astral realms that weave their reality, a truer reality, all through and around us. You allow them to breathe and entice them into sharing their secrets with you. This new comfort within you maims the weed that holds the astral doors fast as you send a signal into the very mind of the universe. This is no joke. You will gain access into the heart of the purest of mysteries, the very essence of being. And this is your—our—birthright.

What if I told you of all the scenes of majesty I have witnessed? From vast alien skies swarming with fantastical craft to Earthly cities engulfed in rocket attacks; from giant, ancient mega-forests sweeping across the Earth to great heavenly spheres rotating in the thunderous noiselessness of deep space. This trove of sensual delight and expansion of consciousness is a sense open to us all. Your astral guide patiently awaits your call.

And it will be quite a ride you take, if you are up to the challenge. Remember, it starts with your acceptance of your truth and the willingness to let go of things brittle and purely customary. For example, I only eat organic food. At least when I can help it, which would be 99 percent of the time. I do so because I feel better for it, and I'm not just talking about my physical body. I grow my own vegetables wherever and whenever I can. They know me, they know what I need. And I don't drink coffee anymore (although I still love the aroma), as I react against it. Certain wines do me in, so I avoid them. When I do drink alcohol, it will be organic if possible, because I feel better than if I drink conventional. But I do like to have a clear mind, so I drink very little these days. And I do none of this because it is hip or particularly clever, or healthy per se; I do it because it feels right for me. And as I like myself, I want to promote myself. Why wouldn't I? Incidentally, organic farming also favors the Earth—it doesn't detract from it, as modern conventional farming does. Yet as I mentioned earlier, my motivation derives from genuinely pleasing myself, not from the notion of being a do-gooder. And as I am one with the Earth (we're both made of the same stuff), it would make sense that we were both to benefit from a cleaner form of sustenance. Simple science, eh?

It's often said that in the face of death, life takes on more meaning. And this rings true for me. Now let me go a step further and put it to you that in the face of immortality, life goes beyond pure meaning into pure being. This is the impact astral awareness will have on you, and it makes life all the more grab-able and truly sensuous—not to mention a wonder in every moment. This, to me, is the essence of being human.

I've read many books about striving (for this or that) or discipline toward achieving your goals. While the notions implied are honorable, once again I question the intention—or energy— behind their meaning. Those labels may or may not work for you. For me, they don't. Striving, for me, implies just out of reach, and discipline suggests a bowing martial artist with a particularly serious facial expression. Which is not a bad thing; far from it. In fact, I have sincere respect for the mastery of energies that accompany artists in such fields. It's the implication of rigidness and unquestioning that carries on the word *discipline*, rightly or wrongly, that repels me. The word or concept of *focus*, which is essentially what discipline entails, sits better with me; I can relate better to that. But that's just me. It might not be the case with you. Do you see what I'm getting at here?

It's not about a war on semantics, it's about honoring what works for you, what feels right for you.

The important thing here is to internalize the process of what you wish to achieve—take it into you, be it, feel it—not to see it fulfilling stipulations that are external to you and that you may or may not live up to. Your astral body is already there, within you. Astral travel or anything you aspire to bringing into being emanates from a place of self-recognition and self-love, not self-flagellation. That is my point here. Forget the labels and know that you already are whole. It's all there. For even just a moment, drop the hysteria the media loves to infuse you with and stop feeding the fear. Sense the all-is-as-it-should-be-ness all through and around you for just a few breaths. *Ahhh.* There it is. *That* is your catapult into reclaiming your powers, and it was so, so easy. It's all about letting go, not adding on.

And this is where self-emptying practices such as meditation and yoga will really help you in priming the astral body. I've found the best methods to be the very simplest ones, those that don't crowd your head with concepts that are too abstract or complex. For example, if you're not used to squatting cross-legged on the floor—as in, it's very uncomfortable—then why do it when you meditate? A comfortable straight-backed chair or a supportive cushion on a couch suits my reasonably inflexible Western body perfectly.

Now let me briefly take you through a basic and perfectly functional meditation. First, I wriggle myself into a seated position where my back is reasonably straight and supported, and the soles of my feet are both flat and relaxed on the floor. I close my eyes and take three deep breaths, feeling the tension release itself from my body with each breath. Then I breathe normally, releasing the tension from my feet as I exhale. And then on to my ankles and knees and thighs and so on, releasing the tension each time on the exhalation. And it makes sense: to exhale is to let go. The lower torso (and internal organs), the middle torso (and corresponding organs), and the upper torso would follow on in the same pattern. Sometimes you may feel the need to stay with a particularly tight area until the bulk of the tension is gone, and that's okay, but I've found it's good to keep this process reasonably on-pace so as not to let the mind wander off in distracted boredom. You can always revisit particularly stubborn areas later, when you're feeling more relaxed and focused. The neck, the shoulders, the head, the cranium, the forehead, the eyes, the cheeks, the jaw: go through them all, releasing them of tension. And the mind—feel it let go. Feel the space between your thoughts. Watch your thoughts and see them float away, like balloons.

Now the fact that you are doing this means you are meditating. You're not trying to meditate; you are actually meditating. And there is a distinction. You see the concept, or the label, of *trying* puts a barrier between you and what you are actually doing. It separates you in its attempt to feed the lack you wrongly and unconsciously believe to be yours. So don't *try* to meditate—simply meditate instead.

I then like to sense the aspect of my mind in each of the body parts also relaxing and letting go. This may sound obscure, but your mind does not only inhabit your head. Feel the aspect of your mind in your feet releasing. Can you sense that? And so on and so on. So you relax your body *and* your mind.

Now this process may take a little while to achieve, but remember, the doing of it *is* the meditation. After a while, it may only take you a few seconds to reach a comfortable level of relaxation or emptying of the tension that normally occupies you. The crux of meditation is for you to realize that the apparently normal state of being that you identify as *you* is actually not you. Just a little release will go so far in lightening your spirit.

When you are relaxed, you're in a great state to play around with it a bit. Why not strip things back a little further? Don't you want to know who or what you really are? Let go of the past, the future, any injuries or "hard done by" labels you've stuck to your forehead. Just allow yourself to be, now. It feels good, doesn't it? "Oh, but I'll forget my chores and my responsibilities and my duties as a parent, spouse, student!" No you won't. They'll still be there when take on your character again. Just let go for now.

And this is your reminder of who you really are. You're touching base with the aspect of your soul that is all through you but is normally just out of view, lost behind the fog of the delirium of 3-D distraction. You're blowing life upon the eyelids of your higher (as in, vibrates at a higher speed) astral self and, in so doing, reanimating him or her. You're actively and literally setting the giant—the god— that is you into motion. Each relaxation or release is a stretch to her or his eternal limbs. And this is why you are here.

CHAPTER 18

Diamonds

Giant (noun): *Astronomy* a star of relatively great
size and luminosity compared to the ordinary
stars of the main sequence.—*Oxford Dictionaries*

This next trip took me about a week to organize before it got
off the ground. I'd recently heard about archaeologists finding
an unusual mix of prehistoric prints in what they had presumed to
have been a stampede of various species of dinosaurs in what is now
known as Central Australia. This, I had to see for myself!

And so I set about my campaign to do just that: to go back in
time and see it. First came the wish, the desire—as I knew it was
possible. All I needed to do was let my body know what I wanted
to experience. I closed my eyes and felt it smiling back at me as I
voiced/sensed my intention all through it. And my body, of course,
knew the news report I was referring to; it wasn't dumb. It knew
everything about me and all that I had experienced. The request was

so immediate and so simple that I sensed *it* (my energy body—who is really the *me* minus any trace of fear, separation, or purely mortal consciousness) embrace the intention and gleefully roll up its astral sleeves in preparation for the upcoming excursion.

Every day and every night I reminded my whole self—joyfully and expectantly—of how I was going to go back in time, to what is now Central Australia, to witness this particular dinosaur stampede. I lay in bed at night giving thanks to my body for the conscious experience of this scene and the conscious memory of it. Within a week I was awakened just before dawn by the familiar hum of the astral engine as my consciousness split from my slumbering human form. As I was lifted from my physical body, I hovered for an instant in the void before internally voicing my desire once more.

Okay. There's dust and cloud, and I'm flying above the scene but very low at the same time. Below me is all thunder and panic and movement. They're everywhere, flowing in one direction, from the bottom to the top of my vision. I'm traveling directly above them at around the same speed, and it's a sea of color and strange shapes. And mayhem. And fur or down. I'm in front now. The largest I see looks like a T. rex but with a very flat, spoon-shaped head. And it's also in feathers of some kind! They all have color, even the smaller ones. This seems so strange. I hadn't anticipated this.

And that was it. The excitement and the colors of the scene overwhelmed me to the point of throwing me out much earlier than I'd wished. I'd not anticipated the sound, nor the feathery or downy appearance of the animals, nor the panic. The intensity of the scene was one of primal fear, and they seemed in such close quarters with each other that it was difficult to study the detail of the experience. But then again, what had been my desire, my intention with this particular outing? Was it not to experience a certain stampede of dinosaurs? And wasn't that precisely what I'd done?

Now whether or not this was the precise scene the scientists had alluded to in their report can never be proven. Do I believe it was somehow connected to the prints and stampede in question? Yes, I do. I feel it to be so, pure and simple. But that is almost irrelevant here. It's not a proving game with tongues being poked about. It's the experience of the stampede that I've taken in. It's the colors and the energy of it all, that I had in no way anticipated in the lead-up. And it was a hell of a ride! Fantastic! I woke up from it absolutely stoked and with the biggest smile on my face. A diamond for the day.

Just a few weeks ago, I was lying in bed on a hot night having trouble sleeping. I decided to toy around a bit with my energy body, throwing my consciousness out of my physical body and into other rooms of the house. I had no particular agenda in mind; I was just imagining my consciousness to be separate from my prone, struggling-to-sleep body, as I found the process always to be relaxing in itself, and I always gained from reminding it (as in my consciousness) of its true, unhindered state. Hovering above, standing next to the bed, sitting on the lounge, lying by the pool looking up at the stars, sitting on the roof … imagining how it would feel to be in these places right now.

Apart from feeling more relaxed, nothing really happened, and I eventually slid into the realms of slumber.

Ahh, lovely! I feel my energy body turning to the other side of the bed and now being lifted ever so gently. I'm going to think nothing and just see what happens. Suspended in the void; so peaceful. I think this is where a lot of spirit/body rejuvenation happens, in everyone, when they sleep. They just don't know it.

Now what? I'm traveling up, but something feels different. I open my eyes to see I'm sitting upright in a small capsule. It's just me. Around me is a faintly metallic pod with varying surfaces and evidence of technology. It's quite a tight fit but not uncomfortable, and I have the feeling that I'm traveling very fast. Lights and devices and print on the curved, pale metal. Nothing recognizable. I feel relaxed, so it's okay.

Now there is a voice. It's that of a female, coming from a speaker in the pod just above my head. The language is unrecognizable, but I know she is preparing me for arrival.

You know, I just don't feel like this now. I don't want to be on a ship or another planet. I don't want to meet another species right now. It feels tiring. So I'm going to abort, return to my physical body, and open my physical eyes. Perhaps another time.

And so I did. After a momentary physical paralysis as I opened my eyes, my body began to reunite with all its Earthly energies and I was soon back, intact and fully functioning. It had not been scary; it had merely been my intention to return to the experience I knew that evening—namely, being in bed on a hot and humid Earth night.

The reason I'm relating this to you is partly to back up my

guarantee that you will always be safe when venturing out of the body. As soon as my desire to return was internalized, I was back in my mortal coil. At least, the process had started to return to normal physical functioning. The reason I make this distinction is that many people suffer occasionally from sleep paralysis upon awakening too quickly. Your energies are in fact astrally occupied but your consciousness is unaware of the fact and has not downloaded the memories of the experience into your physical memory. Do you get what I'm saying? You've been astrally projecting but were asleep to the fact. And you have panicked for one reason or another and not allowed yourself the time to reintegrate your energies more fully into the physical. This phenomenon happened to me a lot before I woke up my astral mind. Now it never happens, as I never panic and I know that I can always return.

When you panic in the astral, as I see many of you do out there, you fly back and take the fear with you. You're perhaps having a glimpse of something unusual, something outside of your known experience, and it may shock you to the core. This will result in prolonged physical paralysis when you return. You see, you're all projecting into the astral. You just don't know it. When I see you there, I try to engage with you, but you seem drunk and with a veil across your eyes. You're generally wandering aimlessly around the place, occasionally having amazing experiences that you can't seem to remember, but more often than not, you're just hovering slightly above your body asleep in all dimensions, astral eyes shut.

What are you really afraid of? Opening your eyes? Seeing what is really there? Now I know I'm goading you here, and that is fully my intention. These realms are so beautiful, so adventurous they'll bring back your childlike sense of wonder, and so very real. Just lose the fear and open the door of possibility just a little. A crack of light, the merest suggestion of an opening, is all it takes for the universe to hear your call and come flooding in. And you'll be safe. In fact, a lot more than that. For it is our home; it is our mind; it is *us*.

✳   ✳   ✳

I mentioned a little earlier in the chapter the process of playing around with the energy body to help you relax at night, especially if you're having problems sleeping. A really effective technique to this end is to imagine you are lying on the opposite side of the body you are actually lying on. If you're lying on your right side, imagine slowly turning your body over onto the left side. You may wish to imagine turning over, or it may be easier to imagine turning under. Try it a few times, very slowly, until you really feel what it's like to do. Don't just see it in your mind's eye (although at first, that's how you will see it). Try sensing your body's energy as physically as you can without actually moving, turning uniformly over and carrying your consciousness with it. And that's the trick: to be able to sense your mind turning over with this imaginary, yet feeling, inner body. The more you do it—as in, repeat the exercise—the easier and more palpable it will become, until you'll begin to feel that you've actually physically turned over. Now you may wonder, "What on Earth is he jabbering on about now?" But let me cut you short and tell you that this can be the most relaxing thing to do. For some reason, to sense your energy body resting on the bed on the opposite side of your physical body is so light and so utterly calming, as it is accompanied by a gentle inner vibrational charge that puts you into an ideal state for one of those restive, rejuvenating sleeps. And even just to lie there, awake, in this position, is unusually pleasant. Try it out, for in so doing, you also begin to wake up the slumbering giant that is within you: your astral body.

Whenever you sense your consciousness in your body, you relax it, as in "you'll feel more relaxed." In the past, when driving or sitting in a train or even simply reading in a chair, I would often switch my consciousness into my body and notice a sense of holding something. My breathing would be short and my body seemed slightly clenched and expectant in some way. As soon as I looked, or rather felt, within, the tension would subside and I would feel a physical release as my breath began to deepen again. And once again, it required no effort to do so. I didn't *try* to relax—it was merely the byproduct of looking and sensing within.

These days, I'm always within myself. I no longer differentiate between my body and my mind. My mind is all through my body and vice versa. And the great paradox is that the more I'm in my body, the more I'm out of my mind—as in I sense my field of energy to be far greater than the mere housing of my corporeal being. Do you see the beauty in this? Turn in, *tune* in, and you access the universe, the very stuff you're made of. And this sense of ecstasy or being really is the default setting within: the permeating, pervasive pulse of energy, of life, of creation. Just as you are constantly giving birth to new cells within, the universe is constantly pulsing you with creative energy. Think about it: creative energy. How could it be any other way? How could we be anything else? And as we *are* this energy—pure and human—and as we are *fueled* by this energy, how could we be anything but creators?

Not sculptures. Not workers. Not providers. Not prisoners. These are *our* constraints that we have force-fed ourselves through fear and compliance over countless generations. The vision of a slumping, carting, enduring, sacrificing, and manacled humanity is merely that: a vision. And a poor one at that! In my view, and the view of the universe within you, it's the wrong vision. That's why you detest it so, for it will out. The creative spirit within you—no, that *is* you—is kicking with both feet, is elbowing furiously, is sweating behind the kneecaps to be freed.

That's not to say that things won't be done or that people won't be fed. Quite the opposite! Remove the gag and the handcuffs and rub the wrists a little, and even dare to stretch out the neck (with the tie gone, it should be a little easier now) and let the giant within you stand tall. And watch the smile, above all, watch the smile. And the eye contact—yes, the eye contact! The horizon is so much greater: an expanse to behold. The breath of life, so deep and refreshing. The giant marvels at his/her strength and ease of movement and sighs the sigh of a thousand generations. Such unbounded energy! For the motives have changed, and that is everything. He/she senses the immortal breeze upon his/her cheek and responds not from duty, reason, or intellect, but from a sense of wonder, of being, of *creation*.

And it will out. In fact, *it is out*. It's all around and through us. We just need to open our eyes to it. Our other eyes. Do you want to? *Are you ready?*

CHAPTER 19

Eyes in the Dark

The alien is lying outstretched and supine on the table in front of me. It has an enormous domed skull, is very tall, and its sinewy muscles and tendons are almost entirely visible under the thin and quasi-transparent layer of skin. It has a deep chest cavity, a narrow long neck, and very thin elongated limbs. The spine is so curved that only the upper back and the pelvis are in contact with the table.

It has such a beautiful and naïve energy, devoid of any taint of deviousness. It is so genuine and vulnerable in its call for help. It wants to know emotion. It is here, on this planet, sharing this body, to understand better and experience emotion firsthand.

This second sight we have—often referred to as clairvoyance—is your astral sight or the sight of your astral body. When you wake your body up to it, you begin to recognize this ability and start to notice things a bit more. These things were always there—you were always seeing them; you just didn't realize it and hadn't made the conscious connection. As the veil begins to lift further, your definition of reality suddenly makes the flip, and what you earlier perceived to be the second reality—the world of energy, ideas, and motivation (the formerly invisible world)—becomes the prime reality, dethroning the merely physical realm to second position. When this happens, you are released from reactivity, blindness, and the default material-world sense of panic. For you now know you are everything, that nothing needs to be added on, and that you are at all times existing in perfection. This is our true and continually present state. And then the clay that is this human life feels all the more sensuous and inviting as you begin to shape your passions and imaginings into being.

Quite a few years ago, I was giving Reiki to a friend with my eyes closed—as I would often do—when I noticed something quite peculiar. In a flash, my second sight revealed her to be reptilian in some way. In absolute clarity, I saw her reptilian right eye near mine and the shiny, leathery, scaly skin of her entire body, and I knew this to be somehow real. Do you see what I'm saying about this otherwise dormant sense within us? All it took was a moment of a glimpse behind the veil to see what was really there.

Now forget the sci-fi for a while and drop all judgment or disbelief as I take you through this. I was naturally taken aback at this vision but at the same time intrigued as to what it might mean. She wasn't a close friend, but I had the feeling I could trust my intuition enough to share with her exactly what I had seen. I had learned to do that: to know when I could tell clients and when I shouldn't. At first, she seemed shocked that I'd actually seen this—shocked enough not to respond for a time. And then, after a deep sigh, she explained she'd been living with this situation for some time now. *Situation? For some time?* You see, she was an extremely sensitive person. And troubled. She had been dealing in other realms for a while and seemed to be playing host to a form of lizard or reptilian energy. Now I certainly do not wish to scare you here; this is not my intention. I'm wanting to point out to you that for reasons really only known to her, she was engaged in some kind of tussle with this other being at her own volition, and my astral sight had confirmed the reality of this to her, enabling her to more fully confront a situation that, as she described it, had been draining her in some way. Can you see the power in this? To see what is there, what is behind the facade of a certain situation or condition? Now she had direction; she had a choice to make. And that would be hers to make.

Apart from the therapeutic application, can you see how fascinating such an unhindered sense is? I have experienced many similar visions with clients over the years and become gradually convinced that it was a play of sovereign energies at work here. What I mean is that I had the feeling visions would be revealed only at the behest of the higher self, the more self-realized energetic aspects of the client. Underlying realities would be exposed if the condition or health of the client would benefit from such revelations. A mouthful, to be sure, but what I'm referring to once more is that strings are being pulled from higher planes. Guidance is at work here—guidance to become more whole and release what is stifling you.

Another woman came to me because she felt she had difficulty understanding and expressing emotions. As soon as she hit the table, I saw it. Clear as day. *The alien.* I'd close my eyes and there it was, lying on the table at full stretch. Open my eyes, there was the human; close my eyes, there was the alien. Not a glimpse of an otherworldly being but a vision that was held, continuously, throughout the entire session.

Now when I refer to the being as "the alien," I absolutely intend no negative connotation. Why would I? Do you? It is without fear, racism, horror, or denigration in any way that I refer to this otherworldly being lying supine on the treatment table before me. In fact, if truth be known, it was with wonder and an open heart that I beheld the scene.

The woman was of a brittle composition: tall, with a rigid narrow chest and a long neck. I did not tell her what I saw. The alien was of a startlingly similar physical build, thinner, taller and with an unusually shaped head, broadening out substantially and domelike at the back. For some reason, I really felt for that alien and that woman lying there in their state of shared and genuine vulnerability. They were on a journey together, these two creatures, whether in her or its life, whether in this or some other dimension, or even possibly in two distant yet coinciding times. Whatever was the case, I felt they were sharing the experience of being, together.

The alien energy had always been within her and was coming to terms with emoting in human terms. She was an alien in human clothing, and both were broadening their experiences of universal consciousness. And she is not alone. There are many aliens among us, just as many of us have experienced lifetimes in other dimensions and on other planets, and are doing so now. It's a playground and a half out there. Would you want it any other way?

A twenty-year-old girl came to see me regarding the depression she'd recently been diagnosed with. She wished to treat it without drugs and seemed resolute in her intent, so we embarked on a few months of fortnightly sessions. She would lose consciousness immediately as the treatments began, and then it would happen. Her eyes would half-open and follow me around the table for the entirety of the treatment. It was quite unnerving at first, as they were not her eyes—they were the darker eyes of an ego within her. Fearing discovery and expulsion, they observed me slyly yet ever so closely.

The girl had no recollection of this happening, yet over time she was to begin to dream again. She would tell me of her dreams that, to my mind, were very clear in their meaning. They alluded to abuse that had been buried within her memories, enlivening the ego to take residence within her. You see, all is energy, and this fear gained nourishment from her unconscious experience of the trauma that had over years come to define her personality. As soon as a torch was shone in, its days were numbered—and it somehow sensed this. Her courage to deal with the past became her hidden treasure as she managed to move forward, deflate the ego, and live as a happier, truer, and freer self. And her freedom came from within—and was real—as distinct from the artificially derived version. Her empowerment was all the greater because of it.

My intention here is not to sell you on Reiki or energy healing but to point out to you both the potential of releasing this inner astral awareness and the implications it entails in unmasking the imposter that so many of us are banking on (figuratively and literally) as the true and only reality. I ask you once again: "What is it you want to see?"

And by the way, all the images, scenes, and experiences I've astrally experienced have etched themselves with far greater vigor into my memory banks than this perceived reality. It really is a state of hyper-awareness that you access, with images and perceptions ultra-vivid and ultra-sticky, in the hard drive of your memory. It's so real! That's why it's the place of *knowing*, as distinct from knowledge. And I believe it's the soil from which all Earthly experience germinates. Soil, earth, clay—it all speaks of creation, don't you think?

✳   ✳   ✳

A teenage girl came to me at the advice of some friends of mine. She didn't know where else to turn and seemed highly distressed. She'd been having frequent dark visitations (oh, I do love that word!) and hadn't slept peacefully for weeks. She was actually in a terrible state. Sleeves rolled up and keen to help, I cleared her energy field using Reiki and shared a few visualization methods that I knew would help ease the stress she'd been feeling and assist her in abating any further unwanted advances of the dark. It helped. Instantly. For the next two weeks, she slept like our cat (which is to say, very well), fear-free, shadow-free, and unhindered.

I later heard from my friends that things had gotten bad again and that she had returned to her former, fretting, non-sleeping self. I decided to pay her a visit. It seemed she had forgotten the visualizations and the approach that I'd shared with her, and she appeared particularly animated in her descriptions of all that she'd been subjected to. As I looked into her eyes, it struck me that she loved it. The whole thing. She seemed defensive about continuing to take measures against the attacks, and I realized in that instant that it was who she was at that particular time—it was who she wanted to be. And I could respect that; I had to. I then asked her if she had ever deliberately delved into the dark arts (or black magic) herself, to which she enthusiastically replied yes. Right. Her call. All I could advise was that from experience, her health might suffer. What I'm alluding to here is that this was *her* reality she had chosen—which was valid in itself—and *her* definition of herself that she had also chosen, just as many of us choose to live in stories and as actors of our own creation even at the expense of our own health.

Returning to the subject of the dark—it is a fascinating phenomenon. What forces are at work here, in our consciousness, that project such strong vortexes of supposed negative energy or fear into our shared, external reality? I've encountered two people in my life whose energy fields have been suffused with this dark energy. On both occasions, I felt something within me cry out when they entered the room I was in. Each time, it was quite shocking. My heart would reach a staggering tempo and I had to contain the urge to either run or pass out while I felt my insides wriggle to free themselves, tooth and nail.

The first time, it was a man in his early thirties. I was teaching business English to a group of around a dozen employees of an IT company situated on Vienna's fringe. He was the last to enter the room, as the rest of us had already started the lesson and were sitting around a large round table. As soon as the door opened, I felt the energy in the room contract as the light seemed to be sucked out of it. The mood around the table instantly changed from one of fun and eagerness and sharing to a furtive morass of lack of confidence, separation, and nonengagement. The group had withdrawn and lost its smile. They perhaps were not aware of it, but inside they were whimpering just as much as I was. Now this was around thirteen years ago—a year or so prior to my awakening—and at this stage I was becoming more conscious of the play of energy in and around group dynamics. But *this* … this was something new, both highly unsettling and absolutely fascinating.

I watched people's bodies slump in their chairs as the *un-energy* imploded all that was good and whole from the room. The golden ball of impetus and inspiration that had initially sparked the table's enthusiasm and lust for new life/experience had retracted to the heavenly hand above, taking all reverberations with it. Time was negative.

The man was quite good-looking, very confident (you could even say charismatic), and had a low and strangely permeating voice that struck emptiness into the very marrow of our being. Yet despite all of this, he seemed like quite a nice guy. When you looked through all that was transpiring on the energetic level—the level of the underpinning and truer reality—he did not appear to be overtly malevolent. But he did have the table in his grasp, and he seemed oblivious to (or accustomed to) his effect on the others in the room. I really had to make a conscious effort to keep myself and the class together. And to leave that room was, *ahh*, such salve! I was so happy never to see him again.

What was this darkness? Where did such *un-life* emanate from? Why, and what was its purpose? Was it his choice to have this or had it been somehow cast upon him? If so, by whom or what? And how would his life be and all those who were involved with him?

I've met many people who were energy vampires, as we all have. And I've met many others with the anti-Midas touch, in that seemingly all they touch turns to rot. But this was very, *very* different. Nor was he a pessimist or particularly negative in his outlook. He just happened to carry the shadow.

The next situation, some seven or so years later, involved a girl of around eleven who I'd been assigned to teach the violin to, individually, in a private girls' school in Melbourne, Australia. Basically the same phenomenon occurred but to a mildly lesser extent. It was the same breed of dark but not yet full-fledged. She was a pretty girl who also carried herself with extreme confidence and observed and maintained her will with people rather than actually interacting with them. Now I'm not exaggerating here. I've been involved in teaching for around thirty years and have had many students in varying fields, and I've never met a child, since or before, with such an ability to make your innards cower and seek urgent cover. And this was purely from her presence—or, in my opinion, *lack thereof.*

You see, I believe these people are born with these energies accompanying them. Antimatter personified. They perhaps exist to give the shadow some air and allow it to play its hand, personally, in the great illusion. Like a magnet that repels the positive, these souls have taken on the arduous task of reflecting back to us all that isn't and shouldn't be. Very strong characters, ironically, they move through the fabric of their life as human black holes, absorbing light and leaving confusion and depletion in their wake. Probably better to avoid them if you get the choice.

After a few weeks and pulling from reserves deep within, I fired the student (I literally said to her one morning, "You're sacked!"). She soon disappeared from the school community altogether.

This is how it happened at the time—and how I reacted, at that time. It's not about being correct. I may react differently now on encountering such energies. Once again, I see the river—rushing, slowing, seeking, and rushing again—as a parallel for our lives, in constant flux yet in constant perfection at all times.

But there exist far more subtle shades of the dark that we encounter on a daily basis. When I enter the average supermarket, for example, I often sense an energy crying, as in weeping. Quite strange! But now I've come to recognize this feeling and act upon it. This started in me years ago, and now when I look around the shelves, I know why. You see, they're all but empty! Very little food, in fact. It's mainly what I would call "plastic food," manipulated through chemical additives and/or genetically engineered produce. In other words, it's not good for you, it's toxic, it's hurting you. "Can you prove this, can you prove this?" I hear, echoing through the concerned frothing of a mass media high and insane on energy drink. Hardly the issue, as many researchers have done and are doing so on a regular basis, yet they're continually debunked by the bully contingent of the fear-mongering, "pro-human-race-poisoning community" of our society. You'll recognize them as those who embraced middle-age a little too early (and enthusiastically), who wear the tie a little too eagerly, and who look overly important while sporting the gaze of the vacuous. Yes, do watch for the gaze! And the belt—loosened around the waist a little too generously, as they poison their own podge and scratch their heads in bemused puzzlement. *Ahhh*, the illusion: such fun to behold, but to what expense?

Thank God (literally) for the inbuilt, foolproof, crap-detecting guidance system contained in all human hard drives: *feelings*. And when your astral body flares into life, these "mere feelings," as many of you may regard them, become the very stuff of being, relegating reason and judgment to the outer bleachers of the spectator. Nice to have them around, they can be harmless enough if they don't get too uppity or clever, but they have no real bearing on the main game. They're simply too external to be that vital.

There are measures you can take to protect your energy field from the advances of the dark, wherever and whatever degree you encounter it in. In the example above, and in many other places of "pure-profit-worship-at-the-expense-of-the-consumer" (interesting word that: *consumer* ... sounds like a posh breed of hybrid pig with an oversized and continually grunting snout/pout), go inside yourself and sense how you're feeling there. You'll begin to pick up on the intent of what's going on. The astral cry is often sensed, as the space is offering you nothing; in fact, it's detracting from you. If there is actually something that is good for you there, you will feel it.

When I enter such places, I imagine white light all around me. Your energy field responds immediately to such a request or visualization, and as it is in constant dialogue with the astral breeze that flows through all that underpins—*is*—our reality, you will sense a palpable reaction in your field. Oh, it is real. Many of you would have heard about this before, and there's a reason for it. You see, it works!

These are very old rituals I'm talking about and very, *very* powerful. For many thousands of years, mankind has breathed the kind of magic into these symbols and rituals that only truth can afford, delivering to us a connection manual of sorts: a connection to the very source. These energies take precedence over—as a kind of short-circuit mechanism—lesser and lessening, non-delivering energies. (Did you know that if you give ice cream to a child out of resentment, the child will eat exactly that, resentment, in the shape and form of ice cream?)

When you enter a huge shopping complex, what exactly is being offered to you? And I don't just mean the stuff. Do you often feel exhausted when you leave? Or depleted in some way? There are so many energies involved here: the sellers' true intentions; the wanting, the craving from customers past, present, and perhaps even future; the integrity of the products themselves—masses of processed sugar, things made by people who earn a pittance for their sweat, so many poorly designed and poorly manufactured products from cheap and often toxic materials. This is what you're generally up against in such places, in our society. So of course in terms of energy, it's a maelstrom, and you will react to it in some way.

In effect, white light seems to put up a kind of barrier around you. You will notice that you'll make far less eye contact with other customers in passing; or rather, you won't connect energetically—as much—to what they're experiencing in that moment. You see, the eyes are powerful conductors of energy, and the presence of astral white light places a protective veil between you and energies that have the potential to deplete you. Now I'm not being antisocial here: of course you'll still connect to those you want to, but you will find your gaze falling short of many people's fields, as distinct from penetrating them, and vice versa.

Then there is the violet flame. Great for transforming anything negative into positive. Imagine a fire, all-consuming, all around and through you. See it as violet. Ancient and effective. A brilliant way to revitalize your field—yourself—after spending time in public places, on public transport, or warring through a day's diplomatic minefield at the office.

The blue light of Archangel Michael is another powerful protective energy shield. It contains a very serious yet nurturing energy. You sense the sword or blade of protection as your field fills with this deep, effervescent blue.

There are many others, of course, and by sharing these with

you my last intent would be for you to credit the many faces of the shadow our reality reflects back to us with the feigned dignity of fear. For it really is all our creation that we breathe and experience. And it is all a hand of the light; as in, it doesn't actually exist. But there are those among us who perpetuate the fear, the dark, for whatever reasons (usually massive and obscene profit), and as much of Western society is presently occupied with fulfilling a mistaken urge to be more by having more or by having to have more to feel complete, it can help to have tools that speak the language of the naked astral by your side. Use them, experiment with them, play with them; see how they make you feel, and benefit from them. By doing so, you actually help lighten the world. And I mean that both figuratively and literally.

CHAPTER 20

A Sherpa in Thongs

Victim: *Origin* late 15th century (denoting a
creature killed as a religious sacrifice): from
Latin *victima.*—*Oxford Dictionaries*

O ne morning I woke up with a simple and profound *knowing*. I
was both shocked and intensely excited at the revelation, as its
simplicity was the very glove of its hiding. However, on that exulted
morning, it hit my face with the ecstatic twang of the underside
of a friendly garden shovel, swung at impossibly high speed. With
a bruised and wondrous smile, my heart and mind immediately
went about the task of absorbing the new paradigm, one that would
change the nature of my relationship with the material world, or
more correctly, the world of material well-being.

A discovery simple enough yet perhaps so elusive to many
of us as the astral realms have been so tampered with, so bent
and manipulated to serve and benefit those who believe they have

something to gain by its invisibility. As when a hand blinds the eyes it covers and then is gently withdrawn the slightest of distances to reveal all its furrows and fingers in blazing clarity, I knew my material well-being was not dependent upon my income.

This was no well-thought-out idea or concept, no affirmation gleaned from a book; it was simply a realization—*a sunrise*—of a truth so glorious and liberating, and one that has enabled the unearthing of my creativity and voice to feel the warmth and breath of a perpetual sun. The release of years, of perhaps lifetimes, dependent upon the illusory bondage of "job equals stuff" was oxygen to my lungs, was expansion to a clamped and suffocating chest and the breaking free of the mud and rot that had hardened and fastened itself around my form and thinking. You see I knew I was truly free to create, that abundance *was* us; it wasn't something outside of us or something we had to get or necessarily earn. Abundance, including the stuff that we need to operate in the material world, is our birthright. As is our health. Its natural state is also well (as you'll note that I didn't say "good" health). Wellness is a given, despite the fear-mongering of a world hell-bent on medication and insurance clauses.

And you're right: it's not logical. It daintily tiptoes its way around the intellect to lie close and hot-blooded against your heart, the only real place of knowing. And it comes from within, the only true place of revelation.

Soon after this awakening, my wife and I were given a new car.

The old one was still going strong mechanically but had started to fall apart physically. I couldn't actually access the driver's seat through the corresponding door. I'd become quite adept at leaping the passenger seat to take command, but always having to wind down the window behind me when exiting parking garages was straining an already injured right shoulder. Plus occasionally, I would have liked to have locked the car. With around 400,000 km on the clock and a mechanic who scratched his head each time he saw the car moving, we knew it would soon be time to send our beloved chariot out to pasture. And we did love that car. Like an old, wizened, and slightly hunched Sherpa in thongs, it hauled us down so many inappropriate mountain tracks in our avoidance of fire and flood (and the long way around), keeping us wrapped ever so tightly in its secure yet slightly dented embrace. It only stopped twice, involuntarily, in its long life: once when we were parked in town (and it started up again after ten minutes of Reiki) and a second time just around the corner from where we lived over an hour out of town. A friend of mine would tell students who would gape in disbelief at its unlikely and disheveled appearance that it ran on faith—and I believe it did. We genuinely loved our car, and I know it loved us. It protected and carried us. All things carry energy. You do know that, don't you? The day it left us was so sad.

But this energy was soon to be reincarnated into our new car, and what a beauty it was! Blue, and out of the blue—we were truly thankful and willing to receive such a gift. Thankful and willing. Could you accept such a gift? Does it feel in any way wrong to you? The universe, guidance, strings being pulled from above—or within.

I didn't earn the money to buy the car, so could I truly say the car was mine? Well yes, I can say what I want to anything. Could I *feel* the car was mine? Yes. There was no moral stumbling block. The car was a car, and when I say mine, I mean it was ours to use. I own nothing in this world; how can we, as nothing is external from us? Sure, on paper it was ours; on a data file in some computer it was ours—yet it exists in its own state, oblivious to the notion of ownership. A relationship exists between us, the car and myself, and that is pivotal, for it is all energy. Can you see that? Everything you allegedly own, as well as your job or your partner, is actually all a relationship to you based on energy. Nothing more, You see, the car could just sit there and do nothing (I guess it could look pretty, but I'm not really one to lust after cars), or I could drive it and let it take me somewhere. And that's where the joy is, where the purpose is: the interaction, the relationship.

So you see, when I say that my material well-being was a given and not dependent upon my income, it is the energy of that relationship I'm ultimately referring to. I know that I have all that I need to exist in this human form, despite the haranguing, the morality plays, the herding, the naysaying, the attempts at imprisonment, and the fear that is strewn across the screen of this perceived reality by the energies of those in suits far too well-creased. Close your eyes now and take a breather from the game of worldly panic, just for a moment, and allow yourself instead to be infused with the breath of life-giving abundance. Know that it is your birthright and things external will begin to change, to shape-shift, to reflect back to you your true majesty and true form, and you will be released. I guarantee it. Give it time and patience and it will come about, and often in the most extraordinary and unpredictable ways.

Now we get back to mantras here—or rather, affirmations (as I don't repeat these over and over). An affirmation for me is hardly verbal. The words are the mere spark of the feeling—or knowing—that is then infused into my being. The important thing is that it must sit well with you. What I mean by that is, it must feel easily absorbable by you. For example, I'd long known that we are all God (as in the Great Creative Energy), but I had a problem telling myself and feeling that I was God. No doubt my early religious training had tainted this knowing with a certain sense of sacrilege. Yet I was easily able to sense that my eyes were the eyes of God; that my breath was the breath of God; that my mind was the mind of God. And then, after accessing these realizations, I was able to know that *I am God*. God is me, and therefore I am God. Each evening before going to sleep, I would let this reality sink into my human consciousness, and it would take all of thirty seconds or so to bathe in its truth. Not that long ago, I would have been stoned or put to flame or tortured to "release the demons within me" for saying such stuff. "Oh, the outrage! The sheer gall of the man!" Forget all that. Just drop it for a moment, as well as the imprint of the palm trees you colored in so expertly those many years ago. The question is, how does it feel within you? Does it sit with you? Is it your truth?

And so it has been with the sense of abundance within me; a very New Age, hip and much-flung-about concept, I know. But don't disregard its message purely on those grounds. The sense of abundance is a fullness of sorts, a wellness, a plumpness, a release of tension, and a knowingness that all is there—an ease and a letting go of the strain of "having to get." If all is energy, then this energy of abundance all through you and around you is the very blueprint of all that must follow in the material realm: the second reality. When you carry this with absolute and easy certainty, your field releases and expands to accommodate this new and ultimate reality. *On Earth as it is in heaven, on Earth as it is in heaven, on Earth as it is in heaven.*

Imagine for a moment, naïve as it may sound, a world with no money or material concerns. (I know, the song—actually, particularly fitting in this case.) Let us say that you would like a certain kind of house to be built for you. Now, as we have no material concerns, there happen to many people out there who love to build exactly those kind of houses you're wanting. Materials? There also happen to be many people who love to grow, shape, and work with the exact materials you're after. Can you see my point? I'm not designing a utopia to defend my case, as I see nothing to defend. I'm talking about passion or the release thereof. A passion for being, a passion for creating. A passion liberated from the shackles of "doing this for that," or "providing for," or "paying off." (How do your cells actually feel about the word *work?*) Human beings are born to and of this Earth, yet we must pay obscenely for the right to anchor our own feet upon our own soil, our own home—the very flesh of our own Mother, no less—both monetarily and in our life blood. Timed labor, away from your home and family, and the infrastructure to support such bondage. And what infrastructure! Enough to keep you in constant distraction (not to mention debt), enough to sate the frothing and grotesque few—who surely are the archetypal Dark Lords, by the way—to whom we continue to acquiesce and obey. Such strange hypnotism. Such a strange and unworldly spell we have un-enchanted ourselves with. Such an insane and suffering trance. Why?

This is no manifesto I'm espousing. Nor is it revolution. It is a holding of the hand a little bit further from your face so that you can actually see it for what it is. And it's not meant to rile you, either. There are many of you who are living in your truth and following your passion and taking breath from an expanded, natural field.

But by far the majority of humanity kneel down to an external and fearful God, and as a result feel exactly that: external and fearful. The essence of abundance is also exactly that: an essence. It is *our* essence. Start to feel it and reignite its knowing within you. Little by little, your field will expand, relax, and unite, and you'll know what it truly is like to be human. Remember, it's not a fight but a release—a surrender to being.

And so each day on my drive to a job that would soon evaporate from my reality, I would feel gratitude for the essence of abundance all through and around me—physical abundance, an abundance of health and vitality, financial and material abundance, an abundance of creative inspiration and the opportunity to express it. Gratitude or the feeling of thanks has nothing to do with being a good little boy or girl. It has to do with being delightfully present and all that gleefully pours into you while in that state. You see, in so doing, you're giving thanks for being; you're owning your existence and thus denying the victim that lurks so close by (and is oh so ready) any kind of sustenance. And as you feel its sinuous and tenacious fingers release their grasp around your neck, you automatically feel this sense of relief and gratitude as you enter your true and natural state. Your eyes clear and you smile within as you recognize the traits of fear, victimhood, and bondage for what they truly are: the facade of a false and disposable reality that doesn't actually exist. Feel and breathe this life-giving truth into you at all times, and you truly will feel thankful.

Just take a look at so many of our so-called stories and you'll see what I mean about victimhood. How many characters in our blockbuster movies are hard-done-by to start with. From *Batman* to *Lethal Weapon* and well beyond, there is the same old pattern of the victim taking revenge. You can see that, can't you? It's become the mantra of a system that is designed to keep you in a constant state of fear. Do you recognize this? Instead of giving you hope, which they claim to be doing, they exist to remind you of the bad out there, of the insanely violent, and that true protection can only be superhuman.

Cleverly, they also depict the system to be so corrupt that you, as a mere mortal, could have no possible hope against the great behemoth that owns you. They bring out the fighter and the outrage in you—to exhaust you and to make you believe that it always was and always will be that way. They cast a queer and warped anti-breed of "reassurance" around a subtly rotting and fear-worshiping mega-system that has supposedly cradled, "educated," and "made" you into what you are. They place their collective palm against your forehead—at a good arm's length, mind you—and have a good old chuckle and a yawn as you punch out wildly and furiously and get all a-sweat while they pocket your money, pat themselves on the head, and continue the cementing of your spirit into an ever-graying and lifeless 3-D shrinking cube—all the while crediting themselves as being our storytellers. Sure, I'm getting poetic, and I occasionally do like a good old comeback movie, but can you see what I'm alluding to here? The contagion of victimhood and fear is so wildly and inappropriately spread throughout our modern stories that we are lost to the true meaning of the superhuman, which is of course, *us*.

Lifetimes of unresolved, inherited traumas have become the fog that is endemic to our so-called normal 3-D reality. Wars, injustices, plagues, and centuries of persecution—both within the family and the state (which in reality are one and the same, as they share the same energetic root system)—have ensured that mortal consciousness is imbued with the energy of fight or resistance from that very first breath so fervently drawn, and as the medical profession's very first whack on your rump serves to remind you. So you can see, and excuse to a certain extent, the persistent and perhaps unconscious obsessive relationship Hollywood, in all its voracious rage and appetite, has with this theme. And you can by now understand how the lower astral realms, those closest in vibration to our physical reality, have been so tainted and so skewered by this negative, emotional overkill throughout thousands of years of Earthly human experience. You see, the fog has become the default and equates with unreal and deceptively mortal notions such as *struggle, effort, work, duty* and so on. But we are more than mortal. We are eternal beings. I now know that.

So you see, there is no fight, as there is nothing *to* fight. But can you accept that, or do you feel somehow cheated? As the energy of the fight continues perpetually once it is initiated—like an ever-playing computer-generated virtual ping-pong game—all it takes is the first serve for the continuum to be reanimated. But by not acknowledging the fight's existence, you instantly disarm it, denying it of oxygen and stripping it of its emotional charge and faux meaning, to leave it floundering, unmasked, and naked in all its brittle and petty ego-ness.

All exists in perfection, as it always did and as it always will. It is all merely a play of energies, a sleight of hand, a trick of our own creation. You can choose to look away and leave the theater whenever you like. I have, along with many others, and the air is so much fresher, so much crisper there. And the horizon is so much broader.

CHAPTER 21

Deus

I can't believe they have followed me back to my bedroom.
All four of them, standing at the end of the bed. Who are
they, and what power must they wield to be able to barge their
way so forcibly into this dimension?

One night, around a year ago, I was in the midst of dreaming
a complicated dream. You know the type: one where you feel
you have to solve something nonsensical before you can move on.
(I think this may be a parallel for what many of us perceive to be
life.) However, I suddenly became aware that I was dreaming and
realized I had the power to let the conundrum go and go astral.
Finding the nearest static and reasonably well-focused object, I
zeroed in on it and felt my consciousness pulled through it and
into an astral dimension.

I'm in a very old, arched, stone-brick tunnel. It feels like it's underground, and the roof of the tunnel meets the earthen floor in an unbroken semicircle. I take off down the tunnel at breakneck speed and see that it occasionally breaks off into two parallel tunnels, linked by small common open sections. I'm able to take the bends at high speed—which is a buzz— and because of the low confinement of the roof, I note that I'm easily able to keep within the realm without losing it to ultra-high-speed.

But there's something ahead of me now that doesn't feel quite right. It's a man in a suit, and he's big, as in he's blocking my way ahead. Ah well, I'll just fly through him.

But I can't—I can't seem to get past him. This is not normal.

Now he looks me in the eye. He's wearing a dark grey, modern, tightly fitted, fully buttoned-up three-piece suit, and his jet-black hair is slicked back over his forehead. His gaze is very intense, his eyes are dark, and he's not moving.

Hmm ... Think I'll wake up.

I woke up slightly puzzled, as this didn't seem to fit into my astral rulebook. Why couldn't I get past him? I linger a while on this question, until sleep takes me back.

"So you're still here I see." As I face him in rising bewilderment, I see three men bringing up the rear from an adjacent tunnel opening. They're all wearing suits of various shades of black and grey and are soon at his shoulder, watching. They're all smartly dressed and muttering among themselves.

"His name is Deus," one of the retinue announces.

Now I'm goggle-eyed and quite frankly scared. I go to pass him once more, but I can't. There's a barrier around him—an invisible barrier. There's just so much unwavering power coming off this guy that I begin to panic.

"Our Father, who art in heaven, hallowed be thy name." Now why exactly I start saying this, I'm not sure, but I felt I needed some assistance, and it was the first thing that popped into my frantic head—perhaps after the experience in the tent? After all, he seems positively devilish!

"Ummm … kingdom come … on Earth! Uhhh … as it is in heaven!" I shoot out most ingeniously and confusedly.

I can't remember the words, I can't remember the words. Shit. I'm out of here. I'm scared!

Phew! Awake. Why couldn't I remember the bloody words?

Whoa! I'm awake, but he's there at the end of the bed with posse in tow! He's glowering over me now while I cough out some more inanities: "Give us this day our daily bread … as we forgive those who sourdough!"

My mind has obviously gone soft here, and he affords the slightest hint of a wry half-smile. He actually seems to pay attention to what I'm saying, as the bits of the prayer that I can actually get out right seem to occupy him and keep him momentarily at bay.

Now I'm stuck. I'm out of words as they close in around the bed. I throw a possessive glance at my sleeping wife (strangely enough, they note her presence too) as Deus leans forward and speaks—or rather bellows—for the first time: "I banish you. I banish you to an *eternity* in *prison!*"

Far out! Far out! Far out! Gone.

What the hell was that?

Strangely enough, I woke later that morning feeling great.

Soo! Deus. Well of course, it doesn't take much Googling to realize that it's Latin for *God* or *deity*. Or perhaps even a *deceptive* God? He was so immaculately dressed, so powerful (enough to seemingly bend the astral current for a while), so slick, and so clear. Was he somehow bad or negative? I wouldn't say that. He *was* scary—or rather, the situation scared me—and his words were such a pronouncement, made with such conviction. *I banish you to an eternity in prison. I banish you to an eternity in prison.* Why didn't I feel worse? Why didn't I feel doomed?

All I can say is that for the next while, I felt very well, while of course still trying to make sense of his message. Like the car in the previous chapter, a message only becomes relevant when its relationship to you is felt or made sense of according to you. On its own, it is irrelevant—and so, over the following months, the gentle unfurling of its leaves were to impact my life like a giant, heavenly sledgehammer.

But let's turn back the clock to a year or so before the suited one's appearance.

* * *

I had been relaxing on a sofa in the spare room, listening to some music through my headphones. It was a cold day, and as I got up to go and make myself a cup of tea, I noticed a change. It was within me, inside my head. A cog had slowed and something wasn't grabbing as it should. There was, I'll concede, a somewhat delicious distance between the thoughts, bordering on the lazy, but just as a second hand irrevocably clicks to its next posting, my powers of verbal recall had drastically diminished. Just like that—and in that moment—my brain had altered.

Over the ensuing months, I became more and more concerned. I quizzed many I knew regarding the effects of age and verbal memory. I was forty-eight and still counting, yet it seemed to my mind an extreme situation to have set in so abruptly and so dramatically, and so early. I would rehearse key words and phrases for conversations in advance, and I would lie in bed going over people's names I knew, in the hope of minimizing that awkward and time-halting stretch of the mind when confronted in conversation. *A brain in bubblegum.* It had become the default of sorts just to jump ship early and choose the simpler, less appropriate verbal alternative. And with it came a sense of defeat and an immense feeling of entrapment and frustration. What had actually happened?

A synapse gone on strike, perhaps? Who knows, and I'm sure there are a plethora of scientific and medical reasons for what I was going through, and that's all well and good. My biggest concern was the feeling of laziness in my brain when I would attempt to recall a half-sophisticated word. Something just wasn't grabbing.

When I looked deeper at the situation—beyond the physical—I started to make out some shapes. Around a year or so before, I had announced to many of my friends that I was supremely content with my life: thoroughly happy doing my bit of instrumental teaching and touch of Reiki and devoid of any further worldly ambition.

And I stood by that. I felt the freedom from any kind of ambition or expectation to be wonderfully liberating. All was as it should be in my life. I'd released my past's failings through surrender, and I truly felt peaceful for the first time I could remember. And for a while, I soaked in that sun—perhaps for a little too long and not heeding the UV warnings that came with it.

It's a funny and curious thing, the comfort zone. I would often dream of velvet-lined coffins in our little shire by the sea in my beloved Australia. And I would also dream of Europe. Constantly. I'd lived there twice before, and the dreams would always involve complex underground train systems, tickets and connections, and finding houses to live in.

My wife's take on my lack of words was that sure, my life was relatively easy, if not under-challenging, and flowing and enjoyable and all that—but that I was lacking a creative outlet. Now I found this to be slightly irritating, as I'd dropped the performing arts years before and was, I believed, becoming well-suited to a dapper civilian life. And what about the Reiki? "Yeah, that's good. But as a creative person, you need to also *be* creative." I could see she had a point. But did it actually relate to my early onset of what-ever-it-was?

※　※　※

Now it's funny how the puppet-masters have a way of doing things. Back to the time post-Deus: inexorably and sure-footedly, from a dimension just beyond our fingertips, a lever was being pulled, and a decision would have to be made.

During this time, I became suddenly and inexplicably bored with my surroundings and my lifestyle. My wife and I both did. I had plenty of time to enjoy the things I loved doing, particularly surfing, which had become a passion bordering on an addiction, but I sensed screws from an alternate reality being tightened or loosened in the most subtle of ways, redirecting my experience of the world and shifting my stance to face a different sun. Regardless of how much I increased my reading or engaged in memory-building exercises, my lazy brain persisted in keeping its feet up and stubbornly filing its nails. Its gaze was fixed elsewhere. And far off, a wind was beginning to blow.

The catalyst came in the guise of a family death overseas, which would catapult us from our familiar, comfortable, not-quite-happening, graveyard existence to a house we'd inherited in a very dry and traditional part of regional Spain, where the economic crisis of 2012 was being felt at its most severe. To sell was out of the question for now, as it would take months to sort out the legalities. No, we would stay and forge our lives anew, trusting in the soil of that foreign and alien land.

And all the indicators were for us to leave Australia. Our cottage and home of the previous seven years, which we'd been renting from a friend, was also up for demolishment, and my wife, as a classical musician, was unsatisfied with the amount of work she was getting. But the place in Spain? Not really to our liking. It wasn't *us*. Nor did we know the language—and they only spoke Spanish there.

We arrived hard. Nothing seemed to work or flow. Literally. It took days to get the heating working, and it was very cold when we first arrived. The navigation system in the car didn't work, so we were perpetually lost. Nor could we actually speak to anyone. Our boxes from Australia had been lost in transit, and it would be months before we'd have an Internet connection. How could one be so alone and so utterly confused in this new and global age? Both of us were in a constant state of bewilderment, yet at the same time we felt utterly alive. What a strange and brutal christening.

It was after only a few days that I had an astral visit from my blonde female guide, who had continued to age in Earth years since the last time I'd seen her. She was sitting in the corner of our new bedroom watching me with a thoughtful expression on her face. When I noticed her there, she said to me after a while, "You're a very precious couple, aren't you?" In the following moments, she somehow reflected back to me our lives through her eyes. She knew everything about us, past and future, including all our foibles and petty thinking and views of the world. She seemed to somehow stream back the illusion of our personal worlds to my waking consciousness, in all of half a second! It was both highly illuminating and unsettling, all at once. She nailed me; she nailed us. She encapsulated our limited way of understanding in a burst of shared energy, empowering me somewhere deep within—beyond the verbal realms—to see my way forward, to make sense of all that had transpired to get us there, and beyond, in that strange and foreign place. And in that moment, I knew what I had to do.

Oh, and by the way—my words were coming back.

CHAPTER 22

Guidance

Guidance is like an eddy. It's like being at sea in a "beautiful pea-green boat." It whips around you (and at you!), caresses you, beguiles you, and nurtures you all in the same sweet breath. If you fight it, you will drown, for it has the power of the universe—indeed, it *is* the universe—singing its song to you, again and again, so beautifully, reminding you of your way and your power.

Oh Deus, Deus, what have you done? Making my easy and cozy life seem like such a prison. Was that your work? Why all the buffeting, and why all the jabbing? And my aging female guide, who's been with me from the very beginning of my astral awakening, why won't you just let me be? And the voices telling me I lead an "unremarkable life," how dare you! And you, that otherworldly, crystalline, humanoid, metallic-speaking, ankle-grabbing, flying freak of nature: why did you show me all those things and take me to all those places? Not to mention the whole "alien" thing. WTF! Did I really need to know all that?

Is it really so bad to be a pedestrian of life, to wear out the elbows of a snugly fitted and too well-worn jacket? Average is nice: it's the norm. My greatest wish as a child was to be just that: *normal*. Neat is good—it fits. The sun shines, you go to work, you be a good person, you do what you're told, and at the end of the day (in fact, at the end of your life), you wipe your hands contentedly, get patted on the back, and are told in a quietly generous yet not quite committed voice, "What a good and dapper life you've had. Well done!" Is that really so bad?

Not at all, if you know your thoughts and feelings. If you're not slightly sickened by a stench so subtle you could confuse it with aftershave. If you don't entertain a rumbling disquiet deep within yourself or deep without yourself that hovers, like an annoying and ever-patient, italicized question mark. If you don't feel a certain numbness creeping through your body and your life that occasionally squeezes you—and sometimes startles you—in those lost and quiet hours before the dawn. If you don't have repeated night sweats. If you genuinely trust the good and honorable folk of the establishment who provide you with your daily bread, your yearly flu vaccinations, and your education. If you're happy to spend so much time away from your loved ones and loved doings, carrying out tasks that make your hair go grey, your mind go numb, and your limbs go flaccid. If you feel at ease absorbing the day's propaganda feed of terror, security breaches, and local bashings, while outside the sun shines and the trees wave, beckoning you to reenter the world and dance with it.

If you like that kind of world and way of being, stand tall and own it. Be the outrage you so fervently believe in. Look serious and laugh only when something is deemed appropriately funny. Embrace society's version of yourself wholeheartedly and, with your right hand over your heart, swear allegiance to a sovereign and a system who only have your best wishes at heart. And God bless you, for you are living comfortably in your reality.

To those of you who shift ever so slightly in your seats, this book is for you.

CHAPTER 23

A Suit-able Ally

I feel a surge of energy engulf me, so much so that I almost pass out. My body shakes from the soles of my feet through to my shoulders and head as it streams into every aspect of my physical form. And then comes the palpable release as it pushes through my pores and into my greater body; to infuse, to inhabit, to take up residence in my being. And I am altered. For this energy is very, very powerful. I slowly open my eyes to see a new world: one with greater clarity, one with more grace, and one that smiles back at me.

And so my words were to return to me in a land where they had no echo, where they had waited so expectantly and fervently in the ether of a country to which I'd had no attraction. Amidst the incessant howling and barking of the local dogs, and a culture and attitude I seemed unable to read, the words rained and rained—and I had no more dreams of Europe.

And so this book grew from a space I never knew I needed. That, if anything, is the very crux of the book itself. Away from the known, away from the too-well-trod, and away from the well-tailored treachery of a glib and precious existence came a spark that I didn't even know I was looking for myself. Or did it find me?

Respite, for the time being, from the material concerns that had normally defined my daily existence, allowed my creative spirit to stretch and breathe and release. Looking back, I'd known this all along. This time was in waiting and had shaped the past to mold the present. Nothing could be surer.

Yet something was still grabbing at my shoulder and nagging at me, and I couldn't quite let it go.

Deus.

But it was to resolve itself soon and in the strangest of ways.

As if in a full circle, we were visiting the very friend in Austria who had been present in the dream pre-astral, where my consciousness had entered the golden ring. She had also been the one to suggest that I was soul traveling when it had all started. She actually reminded me a lot of my female guide.

Having not seen her for almost ten years, I was excited to catch up with her and share with her some of the astral phenomena I'd encountered over the past decade, as well as hear of her experiences as a psychotherapist who was well-versed in the field of "attached energies" and their implications to the human psyche. As we sat there in her renovated sixteenth century *hof* in a quiet Austrian town near the Hungarian border, having talked all through the night, the subject turned to demons.

She had found that these entities often attached themselves to humans and could potentially cause much suffering unless they were transformed, released, or integrated in some way. They could be the spirits of ancestors, ghosts, or helpers seeking their way to exist in the astral fields, the energetic realms that coexist alongside the human experience.

She mentioned to us a transference technique that she had been using with some success with some of her clients. It involved a method of inhabiting the energy of whatever it was you felt was there or troubling you in some way and asking what it wanted. It was then that I related my encounter with Deus to her. She turned to me with her big blue otherworldly eyes and said, "Well then, why don't we just try something ... hmm?" And as she did this, I felt a wave of energy within me strobe up and down my spine a few times, like the anticipation of a dog who's just been told he's about to be taken for a walk. Something was there and had recognized the moment.

As I sat in a chair on the other side of the table that we had assigned to Deus, I closed my eyes and immediately felt his energy inhabit my body. And it was very, very powerful. Our friend began her role as mediator as she guided us through the very simple and effective process. "So Deus, what are you?"

Power.

"And what is it that you want from Greg?"

I want to control him.

Now as this came out of my mouth, I was pretty shocked. This enormous energy was right through me, and with my eyes closed, I was inhabiting another world. It was immensely powerful. And it wasn't me.

It was time to cross the table and become me again.

"Greg, what do you sense over there?" our friend asked, pointing to the now physically empty seat of Deus.

As I closed my eyes, noting that the surging energy had completely subsided from my body on this side of the table, I was surprised to sense a powerful white energy over there. There was all this light where I had expected perhaps something else.

"What does it need from you?"

Love.

The response came immediately from a deeper place within but still surprised me, as I'd become an onlooker in my own transformation. Even the question had seemed unusual.

"And as you send it, this love, what happens to it?"

Now things got interesting. I had somehow imagined that this energy would now diffuse into the higher realms as it was being released through the energy of love (which often happens when clearing dark spaces through Reiki). Instead, something peculiar occurred. I felt the energy in that other seat—that very palpable and powerful energy—slowly begin to merge with my own energy, my own field. My body buzzed, expanded, and altered, taking this new dimension into my being, as I recognized Deus to be my helper, not my captor. How utterly strange, fascinating, and wonderful.

But there was one more question: "What have you come to Greg to do? How are you to help him?"

To help him publish his book, of course. To make sure he sees it through.

Now this was great! For someone who would visibly fatigue in the land of suits and the corporate world they represented, here was his most slickest and suited himself providing the back-up cavalry charge to ensure the job was done. Through the irony and the humor came an immense wave of gratitude for the clarity, support, and knowing that the way forward was assured. That was the definition of true power.

Why did Deus originally show himself to me to be my enslaver in such a dramatic way? I believe it was all about the shock value; it was to get my attention. As you've gathered by now, I was feeling pretty happy with myself and my skills in navigating the astral and engaging with its inhabitants. And Deus was no figment of my imagination—he was there, in my mind, in the astral, and in the room. Unless you have experienced such phenomena, you cannot properly comprehend their reality. He was as real as the last person you have just spoken to. In fact, because of the enhanced focus of consciousness in the astral state, more so. His blocking of my way, his persistent presence, and his manner and choice of words served to get me to sit up and notice. And it did really trouble me at the time, as I was unable to neatly resolve the encounter. So you see, once again, it was the energy of the experience that carried more weight than the mere words said. The intention of the encounter was for me to sit up, get out of my clever astral head for a moment, and listen.

And to write this book and get it published!

And when I say *listen*, I mean listen with my body. For all the answers lie there.

My life truly had become a prison of sorts: it was comfortable, known, and oh so familiar, yet accompanied by a clearly perceptible and deadly slump of the shoulders. On a creative level, it had become underwhelming and tepidly lackluster, almost without me knowing it. An aspect of me had become the frog, boiled to within an inch of its life, yet still smiling the pained and pleasant smile of the mere survivor. And how many of us trade a true and palpable sense of passion in our lives—or wonder—for a jaded breed of comfort? And while within me I was carrying the mantle of awakened human contentment (that truly never wanes once recognized), along with the bubbling, fermenting elixir of the ease of abundance, my spirit— and my body—knew that a life of mere sufficiency wasn't anywhere near good enough. Not anymore. It was time to shine my light.

✳ ✳ ✳

And so to the conclusion of a decade-long campaign of perfectly timed, immaculately weighted, and thunderously real astral gloves to the head that would not only see me take up residence in a far off and hidden land (away from the material concerns of "having to get" for a time) but would also, more importantly, inspire me to create and write this account that had lain patiently and lovingly in wait all along. An astral time capsule. For do remember, it is in these ostensibly invisible astral realms that the world of form gathers up its momentum into shape and substance, just as the ostensibly unseen mystery of Earthly soil provides us with our physical sustenance, our physical home, and our glorious treasure of natural beauty—indeed, the very platform for human incarnational physical experience. Soil, clay, creativity, and the eternal human spirit.

I had found home, for this is truly what I had wished to experience, to see, and to do. And in saying that, I'm not referring to the house or the physical place where I found myself to be; I'm more alluding to the stretching, the sighing, and the releasing of the giant of creative potential—the god—within me. And my awakening into astral consciousness has enabled this innate yet hidden sense to stir and breathe and enliven my human being with a knowledge or knowing that could neither be gleaned from any book nor learned from any man. As a race of truly noble beings, we need to find home— and it will have nothing to do with bricks and mortar, mortgages, capital gains tax, or diminishing investment returns. No. Instead, it will have all to do with stripping yourself of your patent-leather shoes and plunging your deliciously naked feet into the life-giving flesh of our Earth and lover. It will have all to do with ceremoniously defrocking yourself of your ego and its mask of feigned fear and giving in to the unknown and the glee of the sacred, eternal moment. When trust and true faith are inspired by a sun so pure and so immense and so real, then we will slide from our shackles and gaze into each others' eyes unhindered and finally free from the un-enchantment that has kept us spellbound and in illusory bondage for countless generations. And there, home will be found.

So I ask you—and us, as a race—one last time: "What is it that you/we want to see?"

And so this journey comes to an end, for now. It has been a very personal journey and one that has sprung from a motivation of wanting to share with you this aspect and sense of our humanity that has touched and altered me so profoundly and kinesthetically. Everything that has happened in this book has actually happened; it is all real. None of it is fiction. It all exists, and the experiences have etched themselves into a memory that is immensely greater and more reliable than the shifting sands we attribute to the human memory that, according to the dictates of conventional thinking, resides in our mere physical brain.

Know, if you are reading these words, that it *is* possible to realize your creative dreams (and that this book was indeed published) and that you will be guided to their fruition if you choose to honor yourself—your true, perfect self—and open your eyes and ears to the sweet whispers of spirit.

For that is the purpose of the astral breeze and realms: to give you back your rightful crown and the true sovereignty that your spirit hungers for—to be free, to be human, and above all, to be you.

Epilogue

When all around me is in flux, in seeming chaos, in a suffering and joyous world, I sense an enormous calm within. No, more than that; much more, in fact. I sense an inextinguishable and immovable force of being that is ecstasy. It is always there, vast, limitless, and knowing no death. It is as though my body contains no matter, yet contains the entire universe within.

The experience of the astral dimensions has changed me. It has enabled me to live more actively in the process of the present and accept the inevitability of change as it occurs. I have fewer of these outings at the moment, but I feel that is because right now, I need my energies and consciousness to be anchored here, in the physical dimension. And I *trust*. I trust that when I need to be shown something or taken somewhere, it will happen. And it does happen. Most importantly, none of this is theory to me. It has become the prime reality—it's in my cells. It *is* my cells.

Just one glimpse with your true eyes, ears, and touch can transform you forever. Oil to water. You already know it. But you see it as outside of yourself—the divine kiss. However, there is no outside.

These realms can seem frightening and enormous at times, and thumpingly real, but my advice is to tough it out, let your arms slip free from your safety jacket for a time, and experience something way beyond this book. Let it grab you, shake you by the scruff of your intellect, and take you on a hell-ride. (Incidentally, the German word for *light* is "hell.")

Whatever you do, don't just take my word for it. If I were to describe the sensations of swimming in beautiful, cool, clear water to you, would that compare to the real thing? The tears of ecstasy I've shed upon opening my eyes after these experiences have sprung from a well so sweet yet so mysterious in our distracted and despairing age. Please share them with me. Perhaps it really is time to be bigger than who we think we are, to own up to our humanity, and to remove the mask of separation that appears to serve so few, yet in reality serves no one.

As I said earlier, I've been lucky to have had a free pass. That first outing with the light that came though my forehead has been a blessing beyond words and the most beautiful and confusing thing I've ever experienced. It turned my world on its head and caused me so much frustration and agitation at the time precisely because of its reality, because of its *touch*. My very being was enlivened because of it, and from a slumber that I didn't even know I was having—yet, deep down, perhaps suspected. Why was there so little literature or discussion on the subject, and why was it such a secret verging on taboo? Surely there were others who had experienced the same phenomenon, the same awakening through this process and through these realms, as I had.

I was once out surfing alone in an icy southern swell when I was joined by another paddler. After the obligatory discussion of the conditions, he looked at me and asked me if I'd found Jesus.

I thought, *Stuff it; I'm feeling good out here,* and I shared some of what I was going through regarding Reiki and the out-of-body experiences.

"Ah," he responded knowingly, "Earth worship. The devil's domain!"

Hence the silence, perhaps.

My experiences and views seem to offend and outrage many people. Yet huge multinational corporations who raze entire communities in third-world countries and peddle their questionable products in that most trustworthy of domains, the mainstream, continue to be most vehemently and stridently defended by the common social media, not to mention the common man. Humans and individuals *are* actually involved, regardless of the horizonless concrete wall or barrier they present to us. To stir things up, to question, to provoke, to share unconventional yet very personal notions of being, these actions are neither heresy nor anarchy nor dangerous. It's about personal discoveries that allude further to what we perceive to be the human condition. And while some will throw up their hands in exasperation at the crumbling of our legitimate and good society at the words of a marauding and reckless few (while happily downing a Coke), others may yet sense their own spirit stirring in resonance.

The word *faith* needs to be wrestled back from the church, where it's been hidden for so long. It needs to be restored to its rightful place: in the heart of every human being. And I don't mean the watered-down version that is often so limply served out from afar. I mean a booming, heart-thumping, ankle-shaking awareness that is so strong and so real that to ignore its message would be to deny your own existence. How many of you truly feel a sense of faith: for the future, for your well-being and that of your family and community, and for the world we have created and are creating? Do you really feel it? Do you sense it all through you, genuinely, and without having to play the role of a good person in the screenplay of a structured and neatened mind? Does it require effort to do so? And can you sense your eternal being? Do you know it? For this is true faith, and it requires no ideology, and it is within you.

And yes, I have found Jesus. I feel his energy very strongly. Yet it's through nothing I've read or been told—it's experiential to the first degree. You see, it can only be through direct experience. And I've found the Earth and many other worlds too. And I've found my body. Above all, I've found my body.

The river that is me has surrendered to the soil and the rock that steers me. I can sense and smell the open sea in the distance, beyond the valleys and gorges, that will be my rebirth when the time comes to merge with it. But it's a way off yet; and while I do look forward to it, I breathe in so utterly each bend and rush and stillness, with each lingering moment as the bank glides past to meet and farewell me, all at once. I feel its loving caress all the more as I recognize it, too, as a part of me, and I, a part of it. There's no bad weather now: only beautiful grey leaden skies, wondrous torrential rains, magnificent bawling winds, a sensuously scorching sun, and the occasional blissful still. Yet through all the apparent movement, nothing seems to move. And I hang here, suspended from a point in space that seems to be so mind-bogglingly far away, yet tickles just at the inside of my heart, like a great serpent of light, ever perfect and in constant awareness of myself.

Astral traveling is actually all about being very, *very* present. It's not about being off with the fairies or inducing a supernatural state or being a blurry-eyed wizard. I've learned that. When you begin to wholeheartedly inhabit your body, through wake *and* sleep, you automatically spark a natural process that activates your astral awareness, spatial senses, and memory. It truly is as simple as that. Are you awake now or are you asleep? Can you answer that question? The more you take this question—indeed, *inhabit* this question—into your daily waking being, the more you'll take it into your nightly sleeping self, and the subtle tipping of the scales of consciousness will be thrown toward the astral gear of greater experiential reality. You'll actually realize you're not awake when you're sleeping. And *that's* the key! Be here! Be very, very present! You won't be escaping anywhere when your astral engine does kick in. In fact, quite the opposite: you'll see, feel, hear, and sense the greater reality.

And don't you want to see, feel, and hear? And know? Isn't that what it means to be human? "The deadened and jaded 3-D world is all well and good …" Well actually, it's not! I genuinely and passionately believe that it's time to wake up.

Will you join me?

Made in the USA
San Bernardino, CA
15 November 2019

59942747R00139